# IT'S NOT ROCKET SCIENCE

**4
SIMPLE
STRATEGIES**
*for*
*Mastering the Art*
*of Execution*

**DAVE ANDERSON**

WILEY

*Library of Congress Cataloging-in-Publication Data:*

Anderson, Dave, 1961-
  It's not rocket science: 4 simple strategies for mastering the art of execution/Dave Anderson.
     pages cm
  Includes bibliographical references and index.
  ISBN 978-1-119-11663-9 (cloth); ISBN 978-1-119-11664-6 (ePDF); ISBN 978-1-119-11665-3 (ePub)
1.  Management.  2.  Leadership.  3.  Organizational behavior.  4.  Organizational effectiveness.
I. Title.
HD31.A5479 2015
658—dc23

2015020154

Printed in the United States of America

10 9 8 7 6 5 4 3 2 1

*This book, a wondrous exercise in free speech,*
*is dedicated to those who are persecuted for*
*exercising another of life's greatest freedoms:*
*the freedom to choose and express one's religious beliefs.*

# Contents

# Acknowledgments

- A huge thanks goes to my LearnToLead team for picking up the slack for me while I focused on completing this book on time, and for continuing to grow our company at a pace that defies logic.
- Special thanks goes to my wife, Rhonda, and daughter, Ashley, for their support and encouragement throughout the process. You two are amazing teammates in life and business.
- To Shannon Vargo and Elizabeth Gildea at John Wiley & Sons: After 11 books together you all get better and better. We made this deal with one 20-minute phone call: no agents, multiple meetings, or other unproductive nonsense. Thank you for your enthusiasm and for your regard for my time.
- A big thanks goes to Ryan Cota, my friend and copy editor, who came out of "copyediting retirement" to whip this book into shape.
- To our many friends and clients around the globe who make what we do in our company and with our Matthew 25:35 Foundation possible: May God bless you abundantly in your leadership walk.

# Foreword

When you read a Dave Anderson work, it is like having a chair set for him in your conference room, boardroom, or locker room. He can take all of the issues facing leaders, companies, and teams today and bring clarity and purpose to them. *It's Not Rocket Science* is like having a manual for how to execute the daily steps we have to take, knowing these steps constantly change. Circumstances may change but our discipline to execute under pressure and produce results cannot. Dave gives real-time, real-life ways to make this happen regardless of the size or scope of what you lead.

Although there are numerous way to describe what you receive from a Dave Anderson book, inspiration, vision, confidence, and go-to strategies all come to mind. In *It's Not Rocket Science* Dave ties it all together into a process that helps us execute relentlessly on a daily basis. Once we get the vision and strategy right, the only way we can convert them into results is by leading our team with an effective execution process.

As a coach, our team's ability to win games comes down to our ability to execute under pressure. The steps to get to that point are strenuous, complex, and ever changing. Coaching basketball is no different from holding other leadership positions in that it is never easy because change is constant. Dave Anderson has taken the potential complexity of how to master the art of execution and presents it in four very clear and detailed steps. Any leader's job comes down to daily execution that moves you toward winning results. And that's exactly what *It's Not Rocket Science* will teach you how to do.

—**Tom Crean**
Head coach, Indiana University men's basketball team

# Preface

In my decades of teaching and practicing sound leadership principles, I have become convinced that the last thing most organizations need is another goal or vision they will miss because one or more of the following conditions exists:

- They can't execute to reach it; the execution process is non-existent, poorly defined, or inconsistent.
- The leaders mean well but aren't competent enough to get the job done.
- The culture isn't strong enough to align with the vision.
- The team isn't capable of executing at the necessary level; members lack the talent, training, process, or guidance to get the job done.

*It's Not Rocket Science* is divided into parts that will address each of these issues, providing a basic, effective, and actionable blueprint for building a great organization of any size, in any arena:

**Part One: Get the Process Right!** The chapters in this part provide a step-by-step process, master the art of execution (MAX), for effective execution that most organizations lack. When I teach these principles in my live seminars, I'm often told that a structured execution process is the *something* that leaders intuitively knew was both missing and holding them back from greatness.

This part will also introduce several new terms that apply to the MAX execution process. A glossary of terms in the back of the book serves as a quick reference for the new execution language you'll learn in Part One: the ultimate few goals (TUFs), MAX, MAX acts, personalized success profiles (PSPs), pruning, and more.

**Part Two: Get the Leaders Right!** Technically this part should be the first of the four strategies presented, because if the leaders aren't right, nothing in an organization works very well for long. However, because the chapters in this part refer to the execution terminology presented in "Get the Process Right!," it was necessary to place this part second so that readers would have a grasp of the execution concepts and terms I use in this part. This part provides real-world strategies for improving your leadership skills (your ability to shape culture, effect change, and positively affect others).

**Part Three: Get the Culture Right!** This is one of a leader's primary responsibilities. In fact, if the culture doesn't support the goals and the execution process to attain them, failure is all but certain. This part lays out specific and practical steps to evaluate, build, strengthen, and protect your culture. You won't look at culture the same way after reading this part, and you're likely to approach your obligation to shape and strengthen it far differently than you do now.

**Part Four: Get the Team Right!** Regardless of how talented a leader is, how strong the culture is, or how stellar the execution process may be, he or she can't achieve greatness alone. This part presents highly effective strategies for attracting, evaluating, developing, and retaining great people—strategies for building a stronger and better team.

**Rocket Science Rants** Interspersed among the chapters are occasional Rocket Science Rants. They are blunt and somewhat politically incorrect pieces that endeavor to shed a no-fluff light on the subject at hand.

Although the book is divided into four intense parts ("Get the Process Right!," "Get the Leaders Right!," "Get the Culture Right!," and "Get the Team Right!"), each of these parts has a number of brief chapters that get to the bottom line fast and provide you actionable and applicable strategies.

My hope is that you will benefit greatly from the commonsense, back-to-basics blueprint *It's Not Rocket Science* provides for building a great organization—an organization where the right things are consistently done well. Whether you are leading a business, nonprofit organization, military unit, or sports team, you will find the four simple steps for mastering the art of execution applicable and effective.

I invite you to send us updates at LearnToLead via social media throughout your journey in this book. Tweet me @DaveAnderson100: Send your favorite quote, a photo of the book or of you and the book, a thought, an idea, et cetera.

Now, although what you're about to read is commonsense, back-to-basics principles for building a great organization, please resist the temptation to race through it; instead, take your time and get much from it. Enjoy the journey!

# Introduction

Our world, often said to be changing at a pace that is "faster than ever," has created an unhealthy peer pressure of sorts that has compelled impulsive business leaders, ungrounded by basic and foundational disciplines, to get caught up in the "move faster" whirlwind. The result for many has been far more motion than progress: successions of doomed-to-fail fads, phases, silver bullets, flavors of the month, and hosts of knee-jerk forays into follow-the-pack fantasies that drain resources, and confuse and demoralize customers, associates, and shareholders. To be fair, it is easy to get caught up in the "change for the sake of change," and "do it faster and more often" group mind-sets when you consider the near-incomprehensible realities around us:

- Sir Ken Robinson, international advisor on education to governments, observed: "The world is changing faster than ever in our history. Our best hope for the future is to develop a new paradigm of human capacity to meet a new era of human existence" (Robinson 2009).

- "The rate at which companies get bumped off the S&P [Standard and Poor's] 500 has been accelerating. Back in 1958, a company could expect to stay on the list for 61 years. These days, the average is just 18 years. . . . General Electric, [is] the only company that's remained on the S&P Index since it started in 1926" (Regalado 2013).

- In *Great by Choice*, authors Jim Collins and Morten T. Hansen (2011) somewhat apologetically examine how 11 of the 60 companies Collins had touted as "great" in two prior works have fallen into "mediocrity or worse," more evidence that without a principle-centered business foundation that supports sustainable success, yesterday's peacock can quickly become tomorrow's feather duster (HarperCollins 2011).

- Because of a faster-than-ever business pace, our skill sets have a shorter-than-ever shelf life (Thomas and Brown 2011).

- According to *Forbes*, "The average worker today stays at each of his or her jobs for 4.4 years, but the expected tenure of the workforce's youngest employees is about half that. Ninety-one percent of Millennials (born between 1977–1997) expect to stay in a job for less than three years, according to the Future Workplace 'Multiple Generations @ Work' survey of 1,189 employees and 150 managers. That means they would have 15–20 jobs over the course of their working lives," creating human resources nightmares for companies seeking stability among their human capital, to attain sustainable success (Meister 2012).

- "Access to information and to other people is both unparalleled in modern history. Our 'connectedness' is not only to resources, but to people who are helping to manage, organize, disseminate and make sense of those resources as well. This interconnectedness is creating a new sense of peer mentoring enabled by access to multiple levels and degrees of expertise" (Thomas and Brown 2011).

- The rise of entitlement and political correctness within organizations is smothering once-robust cultures. Steve Tobak (2013) of *FOX Business* commented that political correctness:

> is collectivism, which destroys individualism. Competition is bad. Everyone's a winner. Everyone has to be included and treated the same. Singling out individuals as special or unique excludes others, so that's out. Lost is individual responsibility and accountability, the drive to compete and win, the motivation to be recognized for achievement and superior performance. . . .
>
> Everything has to be filtered to ensure no one is offended or gets into trouble. That slows down information processing, waters down communication, strips out critical

data, and dilutes meaning. As a result, it undermines genuine understanding and effective decision making.

Now, here's the confusing part. Finger pointing and blaming others is tolerated, even encouraged. Leaders blame their predecessors; parents blame teachers; society blames victims. It's everybody's fault but whoever is really responsible. That's because nobody is accountable. There are no enemies or bad guys. That wouldn't be inclusive.

- Dr. Ian Pearson, a renowned futurologist, shared the following perspectives on the six most influential trends that will redefine business success:

  The increasing political and economic dominance of emerging markets will cause global companies to rethink and customize their corporate strategies.

  Climate change will remain high on the agenda as companies seek to explore resource efficiency to improve the bottom line and drive competitive advantage.

  The financial landscape will look vastly different as increasing regulation and government intervention drive restructuring and new business models.

  Governments will play an increasingly prominent role in the private sector as demand for greater regulation and increasing fiscal pressures dominate the agenda.

  In its next evolution, technology will be driven by emerging-market innovations and a focus on instant communication anytime, anywhere.

  Leaders will need to address the needs and aspirations of an increasingly diverse 21st-century workforce. (EY, n.d.)

- In his book *The Singularity is Near*, Ray Kurzweil noted that:

  it took 21 years, from 1972 to 1993, for computation speed to increased [sic] 1,000 fold, but only 10 more years to increase again by the same factor. . . .

  Kurzweil predicts that a $1,000 personal computer will match human brain capability around 2020, and will be 1,000 times more powerful than the human brain by 2029. At that point, computers will have a conscience of their own and will be able to learn and create by themselves, without human supervision. . . .

Around 2045, a single personal computer will be a billion times more intelligent than every human brains [*sic*] combined. (Hay 2014)

Whew! How tempting it is amid a world changing at warp speed to abandon solid business fundamentals and seek what's faster, sexier, more exciting, and extraordinary to get ahead in uncommonly complex times, but as *It's Not Rocket Science* will demonstrate, getting caught up in the "change faster just because everything else is" nonsense is completely foolish. The greatest successes in business annals have always been built on a foundation of doing ordinary things extraordinarily well, not extraordinarily complex things—not rocket science.

*It's Not Rocket Science* is an irreverent and contrarian thumb in the eye to the gurus, consultants, and so-called experts who promote the idea that business must revolutionize or reinvent itself continually to survive. It is a commonsense call for organizations to forgo today's enamoring with fairy-tale business enlightenment and to return to sustainable business success fundamentals that have proved themselves true over the centuries.

*It's Not Rocket Science* asserts that we have already heard, have been taught, and know full well the answers for sustainable personal and organizational growth; however, we've abandoned them and chased various versions of New Age business palaver because they deceptively appear more contemporary, and less Prussian; more relevant, and less old-school; more fashionable, and less mundane. This book will present a compelling, no-nonsense blueprint for returning business cultures and strategies to a foundation built on rock-solid fundamentals, not shifting sands. Most important, it outlines four simple steps for mastering the art of execution—for converting your loftiest visions and strategies into results:

1. Get the Process Right!
2. Get the Leaders Right!

3. Get the Culture Right!
4. Get the Team Right!

Although the strategies are basic and simple, they require immense work. This book is your guide to getting it done with excellence.

# PART

# ONE

# GET THE PROCESS RIGHT!

S adly, most leaders do not have a step-by-step process for executing (a specific mechanism to help them convert corporate vision and strategy into results). It is that key ingredient—that missing something—that they intuitively know is lacking but are not exactly sure how to articulate or fix.

Strategy one, "Get the Process Right!," is the glue that will bind the three subsequent strategies for mastering the art of execution (MAX) together. Technically speaking, "Get the Process Right!" should be the strategy that follows the other three: "Get the Leader Right!," "Get the Culture Right!," and "Get the Team Right!" However, because I will be referring to the execution terminology related to MAX extensively throughout the book, it is important to present it first so that you have a clear understanding of how it works before moving forward.

As a matter of priority, there is no doubt that without getting the leader, culture, and team right first, any process is likely to devolve into chaos. However, when the right leader, culture, and team are in place, the stage is then set for an execution process like MAX to lift an organization from good to great or from great to greater.

If a step-by-step, highly effective execution process sounds like what you have been lacking, then you have just found what you've been looking for—dear reader, meet MAX.

# CHAPTER 1

# Why Your Team Cannot Execute and How to Fix It

## The Challenge

Leaders have a tendency to spend immense amounts of time creating goals and strategies. Many mark the start of a new year with a fresh vision to unite and excite their organization. All too often, however, their results miss the mark as the months wear on and the latest campaign fizzles into the most recent failed flavor of the month, so to speak. Why does this seem to plague many leaders? At the end of the day, conceptualizing vision and strategy is easy compared with the execution prowess necessary to convert them into results. In reality, the last thing most organizations need is another goal they will miss because their people cannot execute, oftentimes simply because they were never taught how. Ask a leader to outline his or her step-by-step execution process, and you will likely receive a blank look or hear general palaver like: "We hold meetings, prioritize strategies, and follow up." Rarely, though, will he or she have a series of sequential actions that comprise an execution blueprint. Leaders do the best they can but still fall short of where they could be, and often should be.

## MAX Is the Rx for Execution

Master the art of execution (MAX) is that step-by-step execution process for more effectively converting your vision and strategy into results. The five steps will be covered in depth over the next several sections. Although the following description of the five steps will not mean much to you yet, be encouraged by their simplicity:

**Step 1**: Get TUF!
**Step 2**: MAX it!
**Step 3**: MAP it!
**Step 4**: RAM it!
**Step 5**: Prune it!

MAX is more than a process; it is a skill set that will make you more valuable as a teammate. It is a structure you can take into almost any endeavor, department, or industry and immediately begin to improve results. Similarly, you can use it to achieve personal goals as well. In many respects, MAX is nothing new. Weight loss companies have used similar principles to help their clients achieve results, and many consultants across the continents have taught different versions of these principles for decades. You will notice, however, that MAX is unique in using these five particular principles in the sequential manner in which I present them throughout this section. The MAX system also stands out in that what I present is essentially easy to apply and nonacademic.

The need for my company, LearnToLead, to spend more time teaching execution principles evolved after years of observing what differentiated our elite clients from those who worked hard and had great intentions but repeatedly fell short of their potential. This need became particularly clear as I taught my most popular workshop, the Strategy Summit.

Now in its second decade, my annual three-day Strategy Summit is consistently ranked as our most helpful workshop offering of the year. I traditionally teach this course in the fourth quarter to help clients prepare for the upcoming year. The format is simple:

- The first day covers how to create a compelling vision that unites and inspires the team for the upcoming year.
- Day two covers strategies to reach that vision. I present dozens of sample strategies and teach the implementation principles to ensure they succeed.
- On the final day I teach tactical execution (how to convert the strategies into results).

Because a significant number of attendees return each year with their leadership teams to once again plan the upcoming year, they are comfortable sharing with each other their biggest challenge with the process. Those enterprises that are most frustrated with the past year's results consistently sound the following chorus: "We started the year with a vision people were excited about, and the strategy was sound. We knew *what* we needed to do; we simply didn't do a good enough or consistent enough job of getting it done. In a nutshell, we did a poor job of executing." If you have ever said something similar, cheer up. You are well on your way to solving your execution woes once and for all.

## What's Next?

- Resolve up front to close the gap between knowing and doing. You may *know* many of the principles in this section but still end up missing the mark because you do not *do* them consistently, if at all.
- Embrace consistency. Even if you are executing some of the disciplines in this book, you may not be doing them consistently enough to maximize your results. By the time you finish the final chapter of this book, *every day means every day* (EDMED) will become a valuable addition to your vocabulary and culture.
- Involve other teammates in the MAX journey, because regardless of how great you are, you cannot do it alone. You need others on the same page—others speaking the same language and creating peer-pressure accountability for the five disciplines of MAX throughout your organization.

- Keep an open mind and find reasons why MAX can and will work for you, rather than dismissing aspects because you believe your situation is unique.

- Look in the mirror. Be prepared to look reality in the eye and deal with it. This will be key as we delve into the book's second strategy, "Get the Leaders Right!"

- Understand that no process will save you without getting the leader(s) right, the culture right, and the team right (strategies two, three, and four). MAX is maximized when driven forward by effective leaders, supported by a strong culture, and executed by high-quality people at all levels within an organization.

- Accept that for a process to work, it does not have to be complicated or extraordinary; often, what is simple, concise, and ordinary works extraordinarily well when implemented consistently and with excellence.

- Contemplate the potential difference in results when you, and everyone on your team, are more focused on maximizing results each day through more focused execution—which is exactly what the next section will explain in detail.

## Parting Thought

Most of us have fallen short of enough goals during our lifetime to understand that execution is where results really happen. In addition, common sense tells us that the most effective processes or systems in life should naturally have the fewest steps. MAX, then, in many respects, is simply a structured and sequential set of principles that helps us execute by addressing what we know has been missing from our approach and by organizing what we already intuitively know is best. *See? It's not rocket science!*

# CHAPTER 2

# Make Each Day a Masterpiece

## The Challenge

Leaders often spend immense time giving thought to, creating, and communicating annual visions or forecasts for their enterprises. These are then broken down into monthly objectives for their teams to achieve. These big pictures provide essential direction, unity, and meaning in the workplace. Although vision-casting is vital, the conversation must quickly shift to "*What* must we execute *daily* to get there, and *how* must we do it?" Your focus should first prioritize the *where*, but then be invested disproportionately toward identifying and managing those essential daily behaviors that convert what I call TUFs (short for the ultimate few objectives that mean the most) into reality. Without this specific focus on the *what* and the *how*, you will succeed only in creating more goals that will disappoint because their execution failed.

## Commit to a Ferocious Focus on Activities—the Daily MAX Acts—the Key Activities Most Responsible for Desired Outcomes

The outcome focus versus activity focus imbalance is somewhat understandable because team vision casting and goal setting are fun, and dreaming of new outcome objectives (TUFs) is creative and inspiring. Selecting and focusing on those ultimate few objectives will be discussed in detail in the upcoming chapter "Get TUF!" Determining, discussing, and executing the activities most likely to create the outcomes can seem mundane and often requires deeper thought; therefore, it is harder work than dreaming up goals. Communicating and holding team members accountable for executing their master the art of execution (MAX) acts may also create pain and discomfort throughout the ranks, because changing one's behavior and restructuring one's daily routine is rarely easy, pleasant, or welcomed by the masses. (For more in-depth coverage of MAX acts, see Chapter 5.)

The reality is, to achieve the TUFs you have never reached before, your team must do daily what it has never done before. This includes executing with a focus and consistency like it's never executed before. As inspiring as your TUFs may be, these goals should never be considered a "destination thing," but a daily thing. To that end, a leader's objective must be to create a structure within his or her culture that makes each day a masterpiece—a structure that, when each step of a process is followed, predictably leads to execution success.

I first heard the mantra "make each day your masterpiece" from the late UCLA men's basketball coach John Wooden. Wooden was known for his intensely structured practices that required perfecting basic drills to the point of exhaustion. Wooden famously observed, "It's the little details that are vital. Little things make big things happen" (BrainyQuote, n.d.). Indeed they did; Coach Wooden's teams won 10 national championships in 12 years, including an astonishing seven in a row, and sprinkled in four undefeated seasons for good measure. In the 10 years that UCLA won national championships under Wooden's leadership, their win/loss record was a mind-blowing 290–10!

What follows are three thoughts for helping you and your team MAX by making each day a masterpiece in your own enterprise:

1. *Redirect more of your focus and energy away from desired outcomes and toward the daily MAX acts that create them.* Outcomes, of course, are your TUFs. MAX acts are the maximum-impact daily actions that create them. TUFs, vital as they may be, are the lagging indicators; they show up too late to affect performance. MAX acts, when consistently well executed, take you to the TUFs and should be focused on daily with more diligence than the TUF itself. Frankly, there is far too much discussion in organizations about the numbers, whereas focus given to managing the daily MAX acts necessary to make them a reality is anemic. In Chapter 5, I will discuss more about MAX acts, including: how to select them, communicate them, train others to do them, and hold team members accountable for executing them.

2. *Identify and communicate MAX acts for each position.* We are not talking about 40 things, or 14 things, but instead the handful of actions most essential for achieving the desired TUF: one, two, three, or four at the most.

3. *Establish an every day means every day (EDMED) mind-set throughout your organization.* Talk about EDMED in meetings, during performance appraisals, and during one-on-one coaching sessions. Post framed copies of EDMED in conference rooms or training facilities. Live EDMED, breathe EDMED, walk EDMED, and talk EDMED. Your team will come to embrace EDMED, especially when they see their own results improve.

In the upcoming chapters "MAP It!" and "RAM It!," I will present specific accountability components in which each team member must answer daily for executing his or her key measures, to strengthen focus and positive peer pressure to perform as well as your culture. For now, you may wish to consider that a more ferocious focus on the MAX acts is the next step your organization needs to attain an entirely new performance level.

## What's Next?

- Once you determine your TUFs, create MAX acts for each position.
- Think MAX acts, not just outcomes. Do a great job of managing the right daily activities, and you won't have to worry about the right TUF outcomes!
- Create both a "make each day your masterpiece," and an EDMED mind-set within your culture.
- As you make each day a masterpiece, watch your daily focus, engagement, and results soar, as outcomes are attained faster and more efficiently than ever before.
- As you work to refine your personal philosophy to make each day a masterpiece, it is time to give serious thought to what exactly the most essential goals for your organization are. This ensures that you are resolutely clear about what you are moving toward. In other words, it's time to get TUF, which is exactly what the next chapter will teach you to do.

## Parting Thought

We have been told our entire lives that "life is short," to "put first things first," and to "make the most of your time." We have also discovered the hard way that those admonitions are far easier said than done. Despite our good intentions and strong will, too many days, weeks, and even years have seemingly gone wasted. The simple and structured execution steps (MAX) for making each day a masterpiece simply convert our good intentions into a workable process, enabling us to make a daily masterpiece a reality. *See? It's not rocket science!*

# C H A P T E R 3

# Get TUF!

## The Challenge

Over the years I have become completely convinced that most people do not fall short of their potential because they are lazy or are not driven, but rather because they are unfocused. They spend much of the day a mile wide and an inch deep, chasing too many goals at once, majoring in minor activities, mistaking motion for progress, speed for direction, and activity for accomplishment. As a result stress levels rise, workloads increase, and objectives are missed. To exacerbate the confusion, goal-setting gurus teach that you should set dozens of goals in all areas of your life simultaneously. Similarly, consultants advise you to focus harder on your wildly important goals, when in one's mind, most business or life goals are wildly important. Like the hungry dog who after chasing five rabbits at once ends up tired and unfulfilled, well-intentioned but unfocused people do the same—in many cases throughout their entire lifetime.

## Focus Fanatically on The Ultimate Few

In my master the art of execution (MAX) workshop, the first step of execution I teach in the MAX process is to focus fanatically on *the ultimate few* (TUF). When I speak of "getting TUF," I am referring to

**11**

focusing like a laser on the one, two, or three ultimate few goals maximum that will drive the rest of your organization to its highest potential. These are *not* necessarily the easiest, least costly, most fun, or most popular goals; they *are* those most important. From the 10 or 20 good or great "would be nice to accomplish" objectives, TUFs are the half a handful of best goals that matter most.

We grasp this principle of focus in other areas of our life. We normally attempt to learn one foreign language, pursue one profession, or master one martial art at a time. In fact, if you are chasing five or 10 priorities, are they really priorities at all? Think about it. If everything is important, then nothing is really all that important. No doubt there is an immense amount one can achieve during a year, a decade, and especially over a lifetime; it is not achieved by chasing every good or great opportunity at once, though! In having excess priorities, little will be done with any degree of excellence, and even less will be followed through with consistently.

Here are six thoughts to support the first MAX discipline of focusing fanatically on the ultimate few: Get TUF!

1. *Don't let good or great get in the way of best.* To maximize the principle of focus, your organization should have a maximum of three TUFs. With more than three, you will find your focus, energy, and resources depleted. Until you narrow your focus fanatically on the ultimate few, you cannot progress effectively to follow the MAX process. Use this same narrowly focused philosophy for your personal goals in life's other arenas, and results will soar there as well.

2. *Narrowed focus stimulates discipline, and discipline fuels consistency.* Please reread the prior sentence again very slowly this time, and let it sink in, as it is a vital success principle. Too often, people think they must will their way into consistency, forcing themselves to do what they do not want to do until it is habit. The problem is that while willing your way may work for a while, it has a short shelf life. Reliable and meaningful consistency follows a formula. Once you narrow your focus on the TUFs, you will automatically become more disciplined, because whenever you limit your options, discipline increases. Once you become more focused and repetitive in your devoted pursuit of TUFs,

consistency ensues naturally as the result of greater discipline. This is because discipline is the fuel that makes consistency possible.

3. *Focus means "the ability to concentrate."* The inability to concentrate because your focus is scattered on the minor many or because you squander it on your laundry list of wildly important goals that are less than ultimate, wastes not only time but money as well.

4. *Respect the concept of a true priority.* The word *priority* came into the English language in the 1400s and meant "the very first thing." The word stayed singular for 500 years (*Dictionary.com*, n. d.). In the 1900s *priority* somehow became *priorities*, and with that shift, focusing on what's truly ultimate—what's most important—was lost in the process.

5. *Rules of focus, like rules of gravity, are unforgiving.* If you have ever turned your head for a moment and had it become your entire day or turned your head for a day and had it become your life, then you know what I am talking about. Just as the laws of gravity are no respecter of people, the same holds true if you violate the laws of focus. They treat everyone the same way, and violators will suffer predictable and immediate consequences. They do not care how unique you think your situation is or how busy you are; if you walk off the roof, so to speak, you're going down.

6. *You can have anything you want, but not everything.* Well, at least not all at once. For example, during your life you may endeavor to become a chef, a professional boxer, a pastor, a politician, and a poet; however, it would be unwise to pursue them all at once. Apply this principle to your organization, and your success will soar right along with your focus.

## What's Next?

- Until you identify your TUFs you cannot go further into the MAX process. After you identify them, the next step will be to determine what you and everyone else on your team must do daily to reach them: your daily, weekly, and monthly MAX acts. In fact, if you cannot decide what your TUFs are, then put this book away until you do! No one but you knows which one, two, or three goals deserve disproportionate time, energy, focus, and resources to move your organization and life forward. They are your TUFs, your mission, and your life. *You* have to figure it out.

- Before we get to the chapter on MAX acts, we will need to spend some time in the next section on an enemy of daily execution that has the potential to render your MAX acts impotent: the fray.

## Parting Thought

All who have ever attended a goal-setting course and listed all their most important aspirations have undoubtedly felt the simultaneous emotions of excitement and doubt. They anticipate where they are headed, but are nervous about what to do first and painfully aware they have no plan to get there. Getting TUF simply clarifies what we intuitively have known all along. You cannot do too much at once and expect to do it well, or for long, if at all. *See? It's not rocket science!*

# CHAPTER 4

# The Fray Gets in the Way!

## The Challenge

You may be thinking of how you are expected to execute toward the ultimate few objectives (TUFs) consistently when you already have dozens of daily duties to perform: meetings to prepare for and attend; reports to read; phone calls and e-mails to make and answer; employee problems to handle; training to conduct or participate in; customers to meet, sell to, satisfy, and follow up with; and the list could go on longer than the memory of a spouse whose special day you forgot. In my master the art of execution (MAX) workshop, I refer to this mass of daily duties as "the fray." *Fray* is defined as "a fight, battle, or skirmish" (*Dictionary .com*, n.d.). Sounds like an apt definition of most daily routines, don't you think? Without question, fighting the daily fray is most likely your own number one roadblock to execution.

## The 80/20 Fray Balance

Do not be too fast to scapegoat the fray as your reason for not executing. People do not execute well because they have no process for consistently getting the right things done while the fray rages. Besides, your daily fray is not going away; it is a fact of life. Although problems can be solved, facts of life must be dealt with strategically.

It is also helpful to understand that the fray is necessary. There are certain duties people must perform daily to keep the organizational gears turning. Execution of anything new or important falters when the fray, and all its inglorious urgency, hijacks your entire day and no system is in place for making sure that what is most important isn't completely subordinated to what's most proximate, pressing, loud, or urgent.

Realistically, the fray should consume around 80 percent of your day. Some days require more time whereas others, less. This would leave you 20 percent of your time to execute the vital actions (conversations, communication, strategizing, and accountability) required to take you past your daily routine duties to initiatives that are essential to long-term organizational vitality. This takes you out of maintenance mode and into growth mode.

People get into trouble when the fray takes 100 percent or even 120 percent of their day. Just to keep up, they have to work a day off, come in early, or stay late. Meanwhile, that which is most vital to long-term growth is neglected as it evaporates into the fray. Do not misunderstand; MAX is not designed to make your fray go away or even to help you manage your fray. As stated previously, the fray is a necessary fact of life, and it is here to stay. This chapter's objective is not to teach you to manage your daily fray. Take a good time management course for that. The purpose of MAX is to equip you with a process that helps you execute toward your TUFs while you work through the inevitable and ubiquitous daily fray.

Below are four thoughts to shed more light on the fray's realities.

1. *Everyone working within your organization also faces his or her own version of a fray.* This is why it is essential to take MAX from *me* to *we* by teaching it to your teammates and installing it throughout your enterprise.

2. *It's the sand in your shoes, more than muscle exhaustion, that most inhibits progress.* I enjoy walking on the beach and take pleasure in the sights, sounds, and smell of the sea. I sometimes walk for miles without tiring, as I'm engrossed in the majesty of God's

creation. What does create irritation, break momentum, and derail progress are the grains of sand that work their way into my shoes. The fray is similar. On a day-in, day-out basis you are not likely to get sidetracked by fatigue or big things as much as the minor annoyances that threaten to nickel-and-dime your entire day away. Without a process like MAX to keep you on track, and help you regroup if you fall off course, you work longer and harder but accomplish less.

3. *A bloated fray creates undue stress that can negatively affect other aspects of your life.* When you don't execute well, you have to spend extra hours and days at work trying to get done what you would have accomplished had you been working with a MAX focus. This means you have less time to spend at home with family or friends for exercise, hobbies, and relaxation. This imbalance creates stress. Sadly, you tend to bring that stress right back into the workplace with you, making you even less effective and causing you to work even longer and harder to get the right things done. This vicious cycle robs your life of joy, fulfillment, and achieving to your full potential.

4. *Your biggest vulnerability is the one you are unaware of.* Unless you are aware of the fray and its role as a gluttonous sow intent on consuming your entire day, you will fall victim to it again and again. But as you become more aware of this danger, you are less likely to get off track. In addition, when you do, you are more likely to regroup and get your focus back faster. Those two adjustments, dear reader, are evidence of maturity, progress, and growth.

## What's Next?

- Recall how many new processes, changes, or campaigns you've seen gobbled up by the fray over the years, and resolve never to let it happen again. If you do not learn from those mistakes, you will not grow.

- Recall how many days in your work life where you have left the job exhausted but unfulfilled because, while in motion all day, you didn't get done what was most important; you spent most of your time just trying to stay afloat and playing not to lose rather than playing to win. Get disgusted, resolve that enough is enough, and decide to change it once and for all. Disgust can be an incredible motivator.

- As you read, learn, and apply the MAX principles, be encouraged by the fact that now, at last, you have an effective step-by-step system that won't leave what's most important to chance. Rather, it will build your execution skill set so that you consistently convert your most important TUFs and strategies into results in all areas of your life where you apply it.

- Take your time as you learn and absorb the MAX principles in this first part of the book. Chances are, you have probably raced through enough new concepts in your career that fell short of your expectations. The subsequent three strategies—"Get the Leaders Right!," "Get the Culture Right!," and "Get the Team Right!"—will then help you fully leverage the MAX process for optimal results. Take the time to master, implement, and commit to each step every day. And every day means every day (EDMED)!

- Speaking of EDMED, you will need a piercing focus on the daily activities, the MAX acts, that bring your TUFs to fruition. This is why the next chapter and second step in the MAX process, "MAX It!," is so important.

## Parting Thought

For our entire lives we seem to battle an unseen, unnamed force that conspires against our success. We may not be able to put our finger on exactly what it is, and yet we still perceive its impact daily. By being able to recognize the fray, and learning to execute in the midst of it, we are more intelligently facing an adversary to execution that has been present all along. Through MAX, we are enabled to coexist success-fully with and succeed despite of that daily fray. *See? It's not rocket science!*

# CHAPTER 5

# MAX It!

## The Challenge

Organizational leaders are rightly obsessed with outcomes, *the numbers*, because ultimately that is how they are measured and paid. And although it is helpful to be a student of numbers, the problem with them is that they are lagging indicators. They show up too late to do anything about them. It's like the scoreboard at a ballgame. When the numbers show up, it is too late to change them. They're history. As important as it is to study the numbers, it is far better to be a teacher and manager of the behaviors that create the outcomes. By doing so you're able to intervene, adjust, change them, redefine them, and hold others accountable for them as a means of still influencing the numbers positively before they're history. By staying in the game and continuing to influence the numbers rather than becoming seduced by the numbers themselves, the outcomes that eventually show up on your scoreboard will be far more robust.

## Focus Ferociously on the MAX Acts

In this chapter, I will expand on my introduction of master the art of execution (MAX) acts back in Chapter 2, "Make Each Day a Masterpiece," by providing a more detailed explanation of what

MAX acts are and how to use them as the second step in the MAX process.

After getting TUF by deciding which ultimate few objectives you will focus fanatically on, the next logical step is to carefully determine the essential *daily* activities necessary in each position, starting with your own, to attain them. These key activities are MAX acts. As opposed to your desired outcome goals, which are the results, MAX acts foretell the results. MAX acts are those daily, weekly, or monthly activities that will have the maximum impact on achieving the TUFs.

Frankly, not everything you can do to achieve a TUF is worth doing. Some actions bring you very little value whereas others, such as MAX acts, get you there faster. A common error when strategizing to reach a goal is to list all the things you can do to be successful as you chase that goal. A problem with this approach is that you cannot do everything. You do not have the time, energy, workforce, or resources. Therefore, just as you narrowed your focus on the ultimate few goals, you must likewise more carefully and strategically select the daily actions required to reach them.

To borrow a martial arts philosophy, an effective strategy to determine your MAX acts is to ask, "What are the fewest moves necessary to end the struggle?" Effectively executing MAX acts is all about applying disproportionate energy to high-leverage targets.

As a martial artist, I was taught early on that if attacked, I was to end the struggle quickly. The longer a fight goes on, the more the probability that something bad will happen increases. For instance, you can punch or kick an assailant in a readily available and easy-to-hit target, such as the arm, and do so repeatedly. The struggle could go on for minutes, and you would succeed only in wearing yourself out and making yourself vulnerable to an effective counterattack. If, however, you scoop kick the assailant in the groin, take his or her forward-leaning head, and bring it quickly into your knee a time or two, the attack ends quickly and painfully for the unconscious bad guy. By choosing to apply the right action or two against vital targets, you more quickly and efficiently accomplish your goal. The same *end it quickly* strategy built on MAX acts applies equally well when executing strategy within organizations.

For example: If one of my corporate TUFs is to increase Learn-ToLead's virtual-training revenue by 20 percent over a six-month period, my responsibility would be to identify the handful of MAX acts my virtual training director would need to execute to move us toward that outcome most effectively.

### Sample daily MAX acts might include:

- Make three contacts daily with current users of our product to build relationships, advise them of what is new, offer to train any new hires on the system, and let them know what additional functions or features are coming in the future.

- Make three contacts daily with prospective users of our product to assess their needs, give an online tour of its features and benefits, and suggest a customized training program to fit their organization's needs.

- Personally view a 20-minute segment of the virtual training daily to keep abreast of its content, improve product knowledge, and see our product through a customer's eyes to notice flaws and potential enhancements.

- The virtual training director would then report his or her results on a MAX board (a device that tracks the MAX acts) at our rhythm of accountability (RAM) meeting the next morning. There's much more to come concerning these additional steps in the upcoming chapters "MAP It!" and "RAM It!"

### Sample weekly and monthly MAX acts might include:

- (Remember, the weekly MAX act is an essential activity that does not need to be done daily but that should be executed at some point during the week.) Create and send to all clients a "new content alert" video message, which details the new programs and topics we have added in the month to keep them informed and engaged with our product.

- (Remember, a monthly MAX act is an essential activity that needn't be done daily or weekly but that should be executed at some point during the month.) Conduct a free Web conference with prospective users to show 10 minutes of great content, give an overview of how the system works, and offer attendees a password allowing them to take a complimentary course of their choosing.

What follows are eight thoughts on MAX acts to help you better grasp this second step of the MAX process.

1. *You must have TUFs determined before you can intelligently devise MAX acts.* If not, then you do not know what you are executing toward. If you still have not completed step one in the MAX process, then get TUF. That's where you will need to start.

2. *MAX acts should be limited to a small handful of vital daily actions—three or four at the most.* Although your people may have 40 things to do each day, these will be the two or three they *must* do, do well, and do consistently. In addition, they will be held accountable for their execution the very next day. This, and RAMs, will be discussed in detail in the "RAM It!" chapter.

3. *MAX acts must be selected carefully to fit each position and each TUF.* There isn't a one-size-fits-all act. Customize them to work best for you.

4. *MAX acts may change from time to time.* Your job is to evaluate results and determine whether the MAX acts are still the most relevant, most high-impact activities that can be executed to reach the TUF. As seasons, economies, team composition, competitors, or other issues change, you may need to adjust your MAX acts.

5. *MAX acts may also include key weekly or monthly activities.* These are the things one doesn't need to do daily but must execute at some point during the week, or the things one need not do daily or weekly but that must be executed at some time during the month.

6. *MAX acts should be outlined in personalized success profiles (PSPs).* A PSP is a condensed job description that compresses the normally verbose laundry list of given job duties into a narrowly focused, easily understood, and prioritized list of MAX acts each team member must accomplish daily, weekly, and monthly. PSPs can be customized to fit any position and can be updated as MAX acts change. In the next chapter, I will present you with the tools to create PSPs and explain their potential to affect individual performance.

7. *MAX acts are the ordinary things, done extraordinarily well, every day—and every day means every day (EDMED)!* In American

football, the plays that make the weekly highlight reel are normally extraordinary. The 80-yard, razzle-dazzle, flea-flicker, long bomb for the score. But in reality that is not how most touchdowns are scored. A play that you never see on the highlight reel is the basic and well-executed 3.5-yard run. Yet, if a team completes these runs on each of its first three downs, it never has to give up the ball. It will eventually score on every possession and will wear the competition out in the process. Your job is to determine the handful of 3.5-yard runs for each position on your team, train each player to execute them, and hold them accountable for doing so every day—and EDMED. This assignment should take some of the pressure off you and your team, because it makes clear that you don't have to do anything extraordinary to reach your TUFs. All you will need is to execute the ordinary things extraordinarily well, and to do so day in and day out!

8. *If you are already working hard and falling short on results, working even harder is not your best strategy.* Working *smarter* by executing daily, weekly, and monthly MAX acts is the strategy of choice for hardworking people who wish to move further and faster toward their fullest potential.

## What's Next?

- Start by determining the daily, weekly, and monthly MAX acts most essential to TUF attainment for each of your direct reports.
- Then determine what you'd need to include in your own MAX acts to help ensure your people's MAX acts are done well and consistently.
- Continuously practice, drill, and rehearse on how to perfect these 3.5-yard runs.
- Hold everyone accountable for executing MAX acts every day—and EDMED!
- Clearly define all PSPs, and communicate MAX acts for every position. Remember these are the most vital daily, weekly, and monthly actions to move you toward your TUFs. To guide you in this responsibility the next chapter will cover, "The Power of a Personal Success Profile (PSP)."

## Parting Thought

The number of days people spend exhausting themselves chasing hard after objectives yet still falling short provokes two of life's most common complaints: "There aren't enough hours in the day," and "One person can only do so much." Although admonishments to "work smarter, not harder" abound, specific instructions for *how* to pull it off are mostly absent. Identifying and executing daily MAX acts is something we know we should have been doing all along. By applying the MAX process, anyone can systematically convert knowledge of what to do into the act of consistently doing it. *See? It's not rocket science!*

# CHAPTER 6

# The Power of a Personal Success Profile (PSP)

## The Challenge

The standard job description is normally too broad and general to influence high-leverage behaviors on a daily basis. Although job descriptions are important to organizational clarity, they don't affect enough of what matters most *now*. In addition, they are rarely updated often enough to maintain maximum relevance. As a result, in many organizations, job descriptions serve more as a human resources wish list for desired behaviors than as an effective driver of the daily activities most essential to reach the organization's goals.

## Five Tips for PSPs

1. PSPs should take a broad job description and narrow it down to include a concise compilation of daily, weekly, and monthly master the art of execution (MAX) acts required from each team

member. A PSP can be created for various positions and may even vary slightly among individuals holding the same position. For example, a new salesperson's PSP may initially focus heavily on practicing product presentations, whereas a veteran's might outline a specific number of calls to one's customer base as a daily nonnegotiable.

2. PSPs should be in writing and should be signed off on by the team member. This eliminates misunderstandings and excuses like, "I didn't know I was supposed to do that," "You should have been clearer," or "I can't read your mind."

3. PSPs should be updated as necessary to maintain relevance. As economic conditions, certain seasons, product cycles, competitive considerations, or marketing campaigns change, so may your PSPs.

4. PSPs should be discussed often: during coaching sessions, at meetings, and during performance reviews. Used in this manner, they provide an excellent tool for feedback, reinforcement, and accountability as you coach and measure behaviors based on the MAX acts in the PSP.

5. PSPs should be introduced to each team member positively and as a focus tool to help the person become more successful. Do not present them as a threat of punishment! PSPs are a tool that you should use to help the people on your team focus, get both you and them on the same page, and enhance individual and team success.

## Parting Thought

Job descriptions have always been a sound idea, but most leaders intuitively feel they don't have enough impact on the daily behaviors that drive results. By creating the PSP, you are simply taking a good thing and making it better, more compelling, useful, and effective. In fact, to make it even easier, a sample PSP that you may use as a template has been included below. *See? It's not rocket science!*

## Sample Personal Success Profile

**Name:** John Doe
**Position:** Sales Associate

**Daily MAX acts:**
- Make three contacts to current customers: check on status and ask for referrals.
- Make three contacts to prospective customers: give new information and set appointments.
- Create a minimum of one shown appointment per day.

**Weekly MAX acts:**
- Complete 60 minutes of virtual sales training.
- Complete two practice presentations with a partner on the product of the week.

**Monthly MAX acts:**
- Make two outside prospecting contacts: make introductions and gather information to put in customer relationship management for follow-up.

I understand the importance of the listed nonnegotiable MAX acts and that they are both prioritized and minimum baseline requirements for daily, weekly, and monthly execution. I also understand they are subject to revision over time.

_____

John Doe

# CHAPTER 7

# MAP It!

## The Challenge

Many managers don't display data soon enough after performance to show the team clearly whether they are winning or losing. This can drain urgency and permit poor performers to falter for too long, digging themselves into ruts that eventually become graves. In addition, when results are posted or circulated, the tote boards or other scoring mechanisms used focus primarily on outcomes rather than the key daily activities that create them. As noted previously, people then commonly fall into the trap of confusing the scoreboard for the game, becoming so enamored with the numbers that they don't pay enough attention to identifying and holding people accountable for the daily behaviors—the master the art of execution (MAX) measures—that create them. The primary cause is a lack of visibility around those measures.

## Get TUF, MAX It, and MAP It!

After you determine the ultimate few objectives (TUFs) and choose the MAX measures to achieve them, you are ready to create a MAX board to MAP those measures daily. In simplest terms, although many organizations have an in-view tote board that tracks sales or production results, very few track and post the MAX measures that create them. To increase execution prowess and consistency, you are going to have to provide faster feedback that shows the team where they stand *daily* in their endeavors to attain their TUFs.

As discussed in the "MAX It!" chapter, you will need to give disproportionate focus to your version of the daily 3.5-yard runs that lead you to your TUFs. One of the most effective ways to create the necessary engagement, focus, and accountability around MAX measures is to MAP progress daily on an easy-to-read, widely visible, color-coded MAX board. Here are the traits and benefits of delivering faster feedback on your team's efforts by MAPing it on your MAX board:

1. *MAPing it on a MAX board fosters engagement.* Having each team member post the results of his or her MAX measure objectives during a preshift posting session heightens awareness, urgency, and the emotional investment of each team member every day (find out more about these rhythm of accountability meetings [RAMs] in the chapter titled "RAM It!"). Knowing faster where both you and the team stand elevates everyone's daily engagement to reach the team's TUFs. This faster feedback on each team member's daily performance drives results, evokes emotion, and shakes out apathy throughout the culture. The same principle explains why video games are so consuming and addictive. You instantly see how your efforts create results as you progress through the game. You would quickly lose interest if your score were posted only when the game was finished. This happens to organizations that focus heavily on outcomes and results without giving enough consideration to the daily behaviors (the MAX measures) that create them.

2. *MAPing it on a MAX board creates team unity.* When you can more quickly show team members how their daily efforts are driving the group forward, morale soars.

3. *MAPing it on a MAX board is a catalyst for faster behavioral adjustments.* When you can demonstrate daily on a MAP where their efforts are falling short, the team will adjust faster and begin to find a way to win. In fact, it will be the team members, rather than just its leaders, who begin to create urgency among

themselves as they discuss which courses must be corrected and what has to change to improve the MAP's picture.

4. *MAPing it on a MAX board eliminates gray areas.* In high-performing cultures there is very little, if any, gray area concerning how people are performing. With each team member daily posting his or her results on a strategically placed MAX measure–focused MAP, gray areas disappear and performance improves.

5. *MAPing it on a MAX board elevates positive peer pressure.* Daily MAX measure posting also creates positive peer pressure to perform, as team members work harder to do their share; in essence, there is nowhere for poor performers to hide, not even for a day.

6. *MAPing it on a MAX board creates a culture that celebrates excellence.* The daily posting of MAX measures ensures that the team members performing steadily day in and day out who are often overlooked or taken for granted get the affirmation and recognition they deserve for their consistent performance. At the same time, poor performance is more quickly exposed, creating urgency to get back on track faster.

### *The MAX board should:*
- Include color coding: green for achieved MAX measures and red for shortfalls.
- Be placed in a location visible to the maximum number of team members.
- Be updated daily.
- Display the TUFs, as well as the MAX acts so that the big picture stays in focus.

### The MAX Board in Action

Back in Chapter 5, I gave a sample scenario of what my virtual training director's daily MAX *acts* might look like. Naturally, these activities would be outlined in his or her personalized success profile (PSP), and results on the MAX *board* could be written as follows:

- *One column for* Client Contacts. The goal is three daily. He or she would mark the MAX board accordingly during the RAM, using either the green marker to post three or more or the red marker for fewer than three.

- *One column for* Prospective Contacts. The goal is three daily. He or she would mark the MAX board accordingly during the RAM, using either the green marker to post three or more or the red marker for fewer than three.

- One column for Virtual Training Taken. The goal is 20 minutes daily. He or she would mark the MAX board accordingly during the RAM, using either the green marker to post 20 minutes or more or the red marker for less than 20.

- One weekly summary column for each daily MAX act. Here, he or she would post the weekly totals for each column, writing results in green for Client Contacts and Prospective Clients of 15 or more (based on a five-day workweek) and for online training minutes of 100 or more.

## Celebrate Excellence!

When team members ask why you are posting a MAX board of their results in a highly visible location, reply with, "We want to do a better job of celebrating excellence to make sure our solid performers get the recognition and reinforcement they need." At the same time, you are also saying without *saying* that you want to do a better job of exposing deficient performance so that it is more quickly corrected.

## Parting Thought

Outline the MAX acts for each position on a PSP; then present these and their importance to each team member. Then use the ideas in this chapter as guidelines to customize your own MAX board for use in your RAMs (to be discussed in the next chapter). *See? It's not rocket science!*

## Rocket Science Rant: If You Don't Like What You're Reaping, Sow Something Else!

We live in an age of blame, where more and more people fault external conditions more than their poor decisions for disappointments and failures. These victims don't want to hear that the Law of the Harvest still applies; what you sow—garbage or good—eventually manifests in a harvest of garbage or good. Frankly, it's easier on the ego to shirk responsibility and snivel through life like a pathetic clod of ailments, acting like a victim, growing old but never growing up. In the prior chapters, I have outlined several key aspects of organizational success that are within your control. These are the issues you get to choose and be responsible for, and they are key in determining your success. Following are three of the most essential:

1. *Your TUFs.* These are the most important organizational goals you can pursue. *You* get to choose direction. That means you own it.

2. *MAX measures.* These are the daily, weekly, and monthly actions you will take to reach the TUFs. *You* have the opportunity to execute what matters most each day. That means you are responsible.

3. *The choice to make each day a masterpiece.* You have the opportunity to engage in MAX measures, pursue those TUFs most essential to your success, and say no to the actions, habits, strategies, and associations that would detract from what you must maximize day in and day out.

Bearing in mind these three highly important decisions where you are left in control, consider the following:

- *You are not a victim.* Regardless of your conditions, and in addition to the three choices just listed, you can also choose your attitude, discipline, and character; whether you will listen to feedback or advice; where you spend your time and with whom you spend it; whether you will learn new things; and more. Tough times are not a sentence that you alone have to serve. Every human being has endured his or her share of trials, setbacks, failures, and betrayals. What separates the winners

*(continued)*

(*continued*)

from the whiners is viewing these realities as stepping stones that build character and shape your future, rather than as bad breaks that excuse your mediocrity.

- *Neither success nor failure is an accident.* Although someone may catch a lucky or bad break from time to time, over the course of a career, or a lifetime, you do not succeed or fail by accident. Either you set yourself up for these things or you don't. Author Jim Rohn defined success as "a few right decisions repeated daily" (quoted in Manuel 2013). He defined failure as "a few wrong decisions repeated daily" (quoted in Manuel 2013).

- *Wherever you are today, good or bad, is ultimately the result of past decisions.* And where you wind up six months, one year, or 10 years from now will be greatly influenced by the decisions you make today. There is no getting around it: Right decisions done repeatedly compound success, and wrong decisions, done repeatedly, compound failure. Right decisions are essential to mastering the art of execution.

- *Success comes from doing the right things, not what is easy, cheap, popular, or convenient.* Growth comes when you are willing to give up the comfort of what you want now for what you want most in the future.

- *You reap what you sow.* If you go through life sowing seeds of inconsistency, shortcuts, compromises, and minimum effort, then you shouldn't be surprised when you reap a banquet of mediocrity. You are responsible for your decisions, actions, and results; therefore, if you do not like what you are reaping, quit blaming the world, and start sowing something else.

# CHAPTER 8

# RAM It!

## The Challenge

People in most businesses are officially held accountable for their results once a month, if that. As a result, focus, urgency, and execution are inconsistent most of the time. Because of this, poor performers fall into prolonged ruts, master the art of execution (MAX) acts become options rather than mandates, and accountability is scarcer than soap on a sow.

## Conduct Daily Rhythm of Accountability Meetings

In my workshop titled "How to Master the Art of Execution (MAX)," I present a fourth strategy of execution that is key to accountability: Conduct daily *rhythm of accountability meetings* (RAMs). "RAM It!" for short.

RAMs are five-minute, stand up, roll call–style meetings, where each team member posts his or her MAX acts results from the previous day on a strategically placed team MAX board.

RAMs provide a forum for quickly recognizing those who performed well the day before and exposing those who did not. They are a cultural game changer, especially when one understands the dynamics of reporting to, and being held accountable by, an entire team (peer pressure) and not just the boss. Here are seven RAM guidelines and suggestions.

1. *Conduct them early in the morning, or at the beginning of each shift, if applicable.* When people arrive to work, their focus is often still in remission. A RAM hastens focus, brings closure to the prior day's MAX acts for each individual, acclaims what was positive, exposes what needs improvement, and strengthens resolve to execute well today so that individuals have a solid showing at the next day's RAM. In a sense, RAMs make sure people are mentally checked in, as well as present physically.

2. *The RAM should last only a few minutes.* Don't even sit down. Gather around the MAX board and report.

3. *You do not have to prepare an agenda.* This is a roll call. All it requires is that you call each team member to report and record his or her MAX act result. Applaud those who delivered, and ask for specific commitments from those who fell short.

4. *Make them commit to you.* Do not assign an objective for people who missed their objective; instead, ask what you can expect from them at tomorrow's meeting. Now *they* own the commitment and are accountable for it.

5. *Go green and red.* Those who achieved the objective will pick up a green marker to post, whereas those who missed will use red. Over the course of a month, the colors paint a more telling picture about execution success or failure than 100 speeches on the matter. When red begins to crowd the MAX board, team members will see for themselves where they need to focus; the red board provides feedback and creates urgency more effectively than another lecture from you on the matter.

6. *Do not allow fray topics into the RAM.* A RAM is for reporting results and making commitments, period. It is not the time to discuss housekeeping issues, customer service issues, weekend marketing campaigns, and the like. Do this after the RAM. The fray is already dominating your day; do not let it hijack your RAM as well.

7. *The RAM should be held every day.* Remember that every day means every day (EDMED)!

Benefits of RAMs abound. Consider these five:

- *You and your team launch into the day with focus and accountability.* The alternative is to begin the day in neutral, while your team stumbles around trying to find its way into a rhythm, which could take hours, assuming they find it at all.
- *Poor performers are far less likely to have several bad days in a row.* The power of peer pressure will motivate them not to let the team down multiple days in a row. The MAX board and RAM combination will naturally shape their focus and resolve.
- *Accountability is accelerated exponentially within your culture.* Rather than holding people accountable weekly or monthly, RAMs bring the *daily* accountability essential to execution excellence.
- *Solid performers and performances are acclaimed quickly.* Steady performers on a team are no longer taken for granted, but are reinforced quickly and publicly.
- *Knowing they will post their results tomorrow creates greater focus for each team member today.*

## Parting Thought

Excuses abound for not holding a daily RAM, so keep the following thought in mind before you start belching out your lame loser's limps: *If something is important to you, you will find a way—if it's not, you'll find an excuse.* A RAM is no different. If focus, accountability, a stronger culture, and positive peer pressure are important to you, then you will find a way to RAM it every day. You really can do this. For some of you it will simply mean putting your coffee and donut down for 5 minutes in the morning, doing your job, and doing it daily. EDMED.

If you have defined your ultimate few objectives (TUFs) and MAX acts, if you have presented them to all team members in a personalized success profile (PSP), and if you have positioned your MAX board, then your next step is to schedule one RAM every day. What more is there to say except that EDMED? Get after it. *See? It's not rocket science!*

# CHAPTER 9

# Prune It!

## The Challenge

It is common to overlook roadblocks to execution and as a result, fail to optimize the people, processes, policies, finances, time, vendors, and strategies essential to excellent results. Thus, over time, more effort is expended to reap diminishing returns, untenable situations are tolerated, and obstacles to execution that should be removed are instead worked around.

## Strategic Pruning for Profits

*Pruning* means "to rid or clear of anything superfluous or undesirable" (*Dictionary.com*, n.d.). Think of pruning a bush and you should see the proactive possibilities pruning has to optimize organizations. However, unlike gardening, where the decision to remove a less-than-optimal entity is cut-and-dry (either remove it from the plant or let it remain), organizational pruning has three categories to more strategically optimize your people, processes, policies, finances, time, vendors, strategies, and more. Thus far the four primary execution disciplines of the master the art of execution (MAX) process have been sequential:

1. Get TUF!
2. MAX it!

3. MAP it!
4. RAM it!

Pruning is the fifth discipline of execution and is slightly different in that it is an ongoing discipline in efficiency to proactively improve every aspect of your organization that affects execution. Think in terms of *continual optimization* and you are on your way to mastering the final step of the MAX process.

But first, however, I must warn you about a couple of necessary precautions:

- *You must prune strategically.* Just as you wouldn't prune a bush with a machete, nor should you begin to hack away recklessly at pruning possibilities within your organization.
- *Pruning too much at once can kill the bush.* Prioritize pruning opportunities and initiate them at a pace most conducive to cultural health, morale, momentum, and daily focus.

Below are the three primary pruning categories with appropriate strategies for each:

1. *Stage One Pruning.* This involves pruning that which is good yet does not have the potential to become great—pruning that which, regardless of the time and effort invested, yields you a diminishing return. The key strategy here is to *realign*. In stage one you're not removing anything completely. Instead you are realigning precious resources away from areas where you are getting a diminishing return and investing them in higher-potential opportunities where your limited time, money, and other resources can be maximized.

   *Example:* You have a solid team member whom you value greatly. But, regardless of how much time you spend with his or her coaching, training, or mentoring, you get the same results. It is time, then, to prune away some of what you are putting into this person and direct it into team members who you see have higher upward potential. Another example might also include a task where you're spending too much time for too little return and must realign the time into higher-value activities.

2. *Stage Two Pruning.* This involves aspects of your enterprise that are ailing and not improving. In other words, business as usual is not an option. In this case the pruning strategy is to *revitalize.* Stage two pruning involves strategies, expenses, processes, people, and more that are on the chopping block. If something doesn't change through revitalization efforts, it must be removed.

   *Example:* You have an advertising strategy that used to work well but now brings an unacceptable return. You are almost ready to ditch it but not quite. You'll try one new angle: a new medium, a stronger call to action, or other measures to bring it back to life. If that doesn't work, you know that you have tried everything to revitalize it and can feel confident dealing with it as a stage three pruning item. Stage two pruning may also involve a nonperformer whom you have just about run out of patience with. You can give him or her one last shot at revitalizing through additional training or a possible transfer to a more suitable position. It is his or her last stop before termination. Sadly, mediocrity is dangerously seductive. If you endure it for too long, it can begin to dull your senses to the reality that business as usual hurts! Stage two pruning minimizes the possibility you'll become mired in mediocrity by bringing you more quickly to the decision that ailing elements must revitalize, or they will be removed.

3. *Stage Three Pruning.* The final stage of pruning addresses the aspects of your organization that have stopped adding value altogether and must go away. In the gardening vernacular, these are the branches that are beyond hope and you must *remove* them.

   *Example:* You have a task you should not be doing but still engage in even through it should have been delegated long ago. It is taking you away from executing the MAX acts that would move your organization forward faster. Examples could also be the perennial nonperformer who must leave the organization, the vendor who no longer adds any value, a product or service to discontinue, et cetera.

   The three pruning stages (realign, revitalize, or remove) provide a decision-making filter to help you more quickly assess and address less-than-optimal aspects of your business that inhibit effective execution. With these filters you execute faster and more effectively toward the ultimate few objectives (TUFs).

## Parting Thought

As I get older I find myself pickier about how I spend my time, with whom I spend it, which activities I engage in, and how I invest personal and corporate resources. I suppose part of this is a maturing awareness of how limited these assets are, as well as my obligation to do a more effective job of stewarding them for the greater good. Pruning is a process that can help you optimize every aspect of your business. It also applies to your personal life. It is the discipline of efficiency that makes execution of the other four disciplines of MAX far more effective. Decide now which less-than-optimal people, processes, policies, finances, time, vendors, and strategies must be pruned, and then do it! *See? It's not rocket science!*

# CHAPTER 10

# Don't Mistake Motion for Progress!

## The Challenge

If you have ever been at a martial arts studio and watched a beginning or intermediate student warm up, you probably saw lots of quick and flashy movements as he or she went through the paces of his or her forms and fighting techniques. In fact, the practitioner was likely to have kicked and blocked at a pace that would cause a spectator to assume that this particular karate kid really knew what he or she was doing. However, an advanced martial artist watching the same warm-up is likely to shake his or her head in dismissive disgust. Why? The truly competent understand one of the first tenets of the martial arts: Speed is a disguise for technique. In other words, people who are not proficient at what they do, or who aren't sure of what they are doing, will often move faster than they should to disguise the sloppiness inherent in their skill set. Sadly, throngs of people in organizations—from front line associate to chief executive officer (CEO)—make the same mistake. The good news is that by applying the five principles of master the art of execution (MAX), you won't fall into this trap.

## Sample Common Danger Signs

Despite the best efforts you and others put forth, you will get off track with MAX from time to time. We are all human; it happens. The key to growth is getting off course less often and when you do, to recognize it faster and make a quicker adjustment. Following are some common examples to recognize that may help you become conscious that you, or others, have temporarily lost their way.

1. *A salesperson who rushes through the sales process.* He or she is prone to skip steps to disguise the fact that he or she does not really know the product or lacks the skills to control the customer through any other means than blazing from the meet and greet to the close. This person hopes that if he or she moves fast enough, the customers will not realize that they are witnessing an episode of amateur hour.

   *Good news:* If this salesperson has daily, weekly, and monthly MAX acts outlined in a personalized success profile (PSP) and posts his or her results during a daily rhythm account-ability meeting (RAM) on a MAX board, you'll see far less of this undisciplined and unfocused behavior.

2. *When shorthanded, a manager may hire fast and recklessly to secure coverage, at the price of making obvious the fact that he or she lacks the skills and structure necessary to hire strategically.* Such man-agers use interviewing as an exercise in inclusivity rather than as an elimination process. In their haste, they ask softball questions, decide whether they like the person, and make yet another wrong gut decision that inflicts perpetual damage on the entire team's morale, momentum, and results. After making a handful of such sloppy hires, they boast that they "hired three new ones this week." The managers hope the urgent pace of their undisciplined process disguises the fact that they have the same effectiveness as using a palm reader to hire great people.

   *Good news:* When MAX is installed in your culture, managers are forced to hire more carefully. After all, they must now bring people on board who are able to execute daily, are held accountable daily, and are subject to faster pruning if they do not perform. These cultural realities force tougher selection processes, ensuring that fewer misfits who inhibit execution and results are brought on board.

3. *Business owners whose credit lines exceed their common sense go on acquisition binges, creating the perception that they are growing their businesses quickly, only to fail eventually.* Their unsound processes, mediocre people, and derelict leadership skills eventually converge to create a perfect storm of vulnerability that exposes the rate of their rapid and artificial growth as being built on a foundation of quicksand. As they added more rooftops to their portfolio, they were able to create the illusion that they were competent operators. The reality, however, was that the new points were simply an extension of their original mediocre enterprise, resulting in nothing more than a bigger funeral for their business in the end.

   *Good news:* MAX reveals untold potential within the enterprise one already has, within continually tweaking lead measures, and within the ongoing discipline of strategic pruning for starters. Business owners are excited to slow down and maximize the gold mine they already have, seeing potential that has always been there, untapped.

## Parting Thought

Slow down and reevaluate every opportunity and asset within your business through the lens of MAX. Ask, "Are they being maximized?" If not, you can begin to use the five steps of MAX to remedy the situation immediately. Motion is okay, but progress is essential. Think of a rocking horse: lots of movement, zero progress. Compare it with MAX: focused and intentional motion that consistently creates meaningful progress. *See? It's not rocket science!*

## Rocket Science Rant: The Positive Power of Pressure

I am convinced that in this politically correct and pampered age, one of the most underappreciated words in language is *pressure*. Just saying it aloud can evoke a wince or scowl from those recalling how pressure in marriage, from finances, or from work caused them stress and pain. But without a doubt, pressure is one of the most useful things in God's creation. It gives rise to life—a baby being born doesn't enter the world without pressure. Filthy coal is unable to become a priceless diamond without pressure. Without pressure in the blood, patients will flatline. Pressure creates energy that moves ships, locomotives, and space shuttles. Pressure to perform is also at the bedrock of cultures where execution is effective and consistent.

Granted, there is a distinct difference between a healthy and an unhealthy pressure to perform. Pressure can work against you when it's your first tool of choice to increase production, as you resort to creating fear-based adrenaline rushes any time you need to raise people's performance levels. Ongoing threats and intimidation are pervasive in sick cultures that inept or old-school leaders lead. These tactics eventually diminish performance as beaten-down people comply but never commit. In fact, these toxic tactics are common in cultures where no execution process like MAX is in place and unprepared leaders must resort to bulldozing their way to results.

On the other hand, in a high-performing culture, pressure is a fixed culture asset that consistently raises levels of alertness, urgency, and performance. Expectations are clear and high; feedback is fast and honest; accountability is swift, firm, and fair; and driven and talented people routinely push everyone, including themselves, to excel. All of these cultural advantages manifest when you implement MAX. In fact, MAX does a lot of your work for you:

- Team members already know what's most important each day, because the MAX measures have been clearly established and outlined in PSPs.
- Accountability happens every day without you having to be the bad guy, because the daily RAM does that for you.

- Pressure to perform is ongoing by virtue of the MAX board and daily RAM. You do not have to give daily battle cries or pep talks to focus people on doing their jobs.
- Less-than-optimal people, processes, strategies, expenditures, activities, vendors, and more are continually pruned to clear way for more effective execution and robust performance.

Granted, even in great cultures there is occasional unhealthy pressure, but the healthy pressure is what dominates day in and day out.

To further support the positive power of pressure—and despite this book's title—I am going to present just a dash of rocket science: the Second Law of Thermodynamics. It applies incredibly well to organizations and clearly explains why you need to drop your wimpy, whiney, spineless objections to the cultural pressure to perform. Here it is: *Things naturally wind down rather than up, unless outside energy is applied (RationalWiki* 2015). This is true in your or any other organization. Things—such as momentum, energy levels, and results—will not naturally wind up. They will naturally go away unless outside energy is applied. As a leader *you* are supposed to be that outside energy, and MAX is your greatest ally to make it happen. Cherish pressure. Seek it. Embrace it. You will not survive without it.

# Part One Summary

An effective execution process is commonly the missing link preventing organizations with strong leadership, culture, and teams from reaching their potential. Master the art of execution (MAX), when installed completely and used consistently well, ties the five strategies for mastering execution together. You now have the outline for a skill set that can make you more valuable and will help you add more value in any position or industry, and that you can use to reap greater rewards as you pursue your personal goals as well:

1. Get TUF!
2. MAX It!
3. MAP It!
4. RAM It!
5. Prune It!

This MAX process requires changing your focus, thinking, and behaviors. It may also create discomfort as it intensely focuses behaviors and lays bare individual performances, all while strengthening accountability on a daily basis. Any ensuing discomfort or pain a new process like MAX brings on serves you well, because pain and discomfort are both essential to growth. People don't grow in a comfort zone—they plateau. Besides, the discomfort and pain a new execution process brings on pales in comparison with the ongoing agony of missing one's potential and of eventual mediocrity. It's painful either way, so pick your poison. As Jim Rohn said, "You can either choose the pain of discipline or the pain of regret" (quoted in Manuel 2013).

Once you get the leaders, culture, and team right, you are positioned to maximize any process, and MAX is no exception. On the other hand, without getting the leaders, culture, and team right, even the best processes are marginalized. Going forward, keep the following in mind concerning the roles of each of the four key entities of execution:

- The leaders are responsible for shaping the culture, attracting the right people, and implementing the right processes.
- Culture assists in attracting the right people and determines the behaviors and results they produce. It also must support any process for it to be effective.
- A team, when working within the disciplines of an effective execution process supported by both strong leadership and culture, will consistently execute over their heads. Without a doubt, the combination of right leader, culture, team, and process creates a perfect storm of force-multiplying results that consistently leads to optimal performance.

However, the weakest link in any of the four strategies for mastering the art of execution will determine the overall effectiveness of the others. All four strategies need consistent infusions of attention, time, and resources to offset the natural pull of complacency and entropy. Ultimately, this responsibility lies with the leader. Your speed will determine the organization's speed; when you catch cold, it will come down with pneumonia. Just so we keep it real: if your culture, team, or process gets off track, *you* are the problem. Do not look out the window for blame. Gaze in the mirror and take responsibility. Then fix it. *See? It's not rocket science!*

# PART TWO

# GET THE LEADERS RIGHT!

Ultimately, the leaders in an organization own the execution process. They get paid for achieving the ultimate few objectives (TUFs) but are likewise responsible when the efforts fall short. Several common obstacles create execution failure for leaders. Here are a few of the most common:

- A nonexistent or ineffective execution process (Strategy one, "Get the Process Right!," remedies this).
- A culture that does not support execution (Strategy three, "Get the Culture Right!," remedies this).
- The leaders don't have a team that can execute (Strategy four, "Get the Team Right!," remedies this).
- The leaders overmanage and underlead.
- The leader is personally undisciplined or unfocused.
- The leader does not take responsibility for results.
- The team has not bought into the leader or his or her system; members comply but don't commit.
- The leader has a flawed leadership philosophy.

This second strategy will address these and other causes of execution failure and will likewise strike at the root of the problem: the leadership of a team. Until the leaders are right, the culture, team, and process will falter. The old saw is true: *A fish rots at the head.* In other words, when an organization is working at less-than-optimal levels, you do not prioritize to fix it in the middle or at the bottom. *It starts to stink at the top first.* The good news is that as a leader, if you face this issue, you can fix it. The bad news is that failing to acknowledge leadership's role in execution failure ensures that nothing changes—except perhaps leaders' jobs, when they are no longer employed where they are currently because they failed to get the job done.

# 11

# Do You
# Overmanage and
# Underlead?

## The Challenge

One of the most common mistakes preventing a manager from reaching his or her potential is to overmanage and underlead. A surprising number of the leaders I have met don't even realize that there is a difference between management and leadership. Neither do they grasp that developing a balance of both skill sets is essential if they want to create a high-performing culture, build an outstanding team, and master the art of execution (MAX). Although I cannot explain as well in a few pages what takes me hours to cover in my *Up Your Business* seminar, I will outline a handful of key differences between management and leadership to improve both your appreciation for and perspective of the roles each plays in an organization's success. Evaluate your own tendencies, and determine which adjustments you should make to help you get the leaders right in your organization, starting with you.

## Paperwork versus People Work—The *Stuff* versus the Team

Although it may seem like an oversimplification, here is perhaps the cleanest way to summarize the difference between management and leadership: Management is about paperwork whereas leadership is about people work. Management involves working with *stuff*. Leadership involves building and developing the team. Do not misunderstand what I am saying. Solid management and leadership are both equally important to the health of an organization. If you have great management but poor leadership, you won't grow what you keep; on the other hand, if you have great leadership but poor management, you won't keep what you grow. It's when leaders spend more time with the *stuff* than they do with the people that execution falters, because the team is likely to be underdeveloped, micromanaged, and overwhelmed.

Management's focus involves systems, controls, budgets, forecasting, scheduling, processes, and procedures. Conversely, the focus of leadership is to attract and develop talent; to motivate them and hold them accountable; to shape culture; to define mission, vision, and values; as well as to create the conditions for the team to succeed in the leader's absence. A healthy balance of both management and leadership is essential to optimizing your results; however, the sad fact is that too many managers overmanage and underlead, because frankly, it's easier. After all, when you are working with stuff all day, you feel in control. Stuff is easier to master because it doesn't talk back; doesn't have personal problems; and doesn't need to be trained, motivated, or held accountable. When all is said and done, because people are messy, managers with weak leadership skills engage their time where they meet less resistance and feel more in control—with the stuff.

Another problem that creates a management/leadership imbalance is that many people in leadership positions have been trained more heavily in the *stuff* aspects of the job and less so in how to lead. The good news is that leadership can be developed. Regardless of how poorly people may be doing, they can learn to do a better job of getting more done through people, as they grow people. If you haven't read my book *Up Your Business: 7 Steps to Fix, Build, or Stretch Your Organization* (John Wiley & Sons 2007), that would be the place to start until you can make it to one of my live workshops where we really delve into the topic.

## The Biggest Problem with Leaders

In my observations, the biggest problem with leaders is that they do not lead. This goes for the heads of nations, businesses, nonprofits, sports teams, and families. Rather than lead, they tweak, tinker, tamper, manage, massage, maintain, administer, and preside. They seem to think that they can build a team by memo, text message, voice mail, or e-mail. Many have deluded themselves into believing their leadership title somehow makes them a leader. What follows are eight thoughts on leadership that I hope will put into perspective what real leadership is about:

1. A title does not make anyone a leader. A title merely buys one the time to become a leader—to get the job done or to blow it, to earn influence or to lose it.

2. No one has ever been made more competent by virtue of a change in title.

3. Leadership is performance, not position. It is a choice you make, not a place at the head of a table where you sit.

4. Leaders do not automatically have committed followers; they have compliant subordinates. How they act as leaders determines whether they are able to convert the *just enough to get by* subordinate into a *run through a wall for you* follower.

5. Followers will not buy into a leader's ultimate few objectives (TUFs) or execution process until they first buy into the leader.

6. As outlined in my book *How to Run Your Business by THE BOOK* (John Wiley & Sons 2011), the number one cause of leadership failure is pride. Every other ostensible cause finds its root in some aspect of pride or ego.

7. The quality of the leader determines the quality of people he or she is able to attract and develop. The team is ultimately made in the leader's image.

8. The number one obligation of a leader is to grow—grow himself or herself, grow the team, and grow the organization together with his or her team.

## Parting Thought

In the next chapter I will present three key differences between management and leadership tendencies, which will afford you the chance to evaluate your own daily leadership style and make necessary adjustments. For now, let me close with the following perspectives. *Leadership* is defined as "the position or function of a leader, a person who guides or directs a group" (*Dictionary.com*, n.d.). The definition of *manage* is "to handle, direct, govern or control in action or use" (*Dictionary.com*, n.d.). These definitions make clear the distinction between and necessity of both skill sets: People must be led, and things should be administered. Almost all leaders get off track from time to time and as a result, overmanage and underlead. A key to growth is becoming more aware of the necessary balance, not only so that you fall off track less often, but also, when you do stray, to recognize it and adjust faster. Accomplishing these two objectives will help you outexecute and run circles around the poor and hapless fools who don't even realize they are off track in the first place. Simple and basic self-awareness, in this regard, is a leadership game changer. *See? It's not rocket science!*

# CHAPTER 12

# Stretching, Trenches, and Changing

### The Challenge

Many leaders fall for the notion that once they create the ultimate few objectives (TUFs) and help devise strategy, execution becomes the team's responsibility and problem. Much like the candidate on election night who holes up in a war room to monitor results, they become passive and wait for the numbers to come in. They spend their days dazed by data, numbed by numbers, immersed in e-mails, and fazed by phone calls, all the while collecting more calluses on their backsides than on their feet and hands. The following three concepts are taken from the eight key differences between—and tendencies of—managers and leaders, which I discuss in my *Up Your Business* seminars. These help attendees become more aware of what they are doing well and where they need to make adjustments in their daily leadership approach. These three are *big*. As you read them, consider how the people who work with you most would grade you (A through F) in each area:

## Leaders Are in the Stretching Business!

1. *Managers maintain, whereas leaders stretch.* Managers are adept at maintaining people, but they're not great at growing them because they don't spend enough time with them. Many were never trained how to evaluate or develop human capital in the first place. They do not seem to realize that although you can impress people at a distance from the safety and comfort of your office, to affect people, you must get up close and pour yourself into them.

   Leaders, on the other hand, are committed to leaving their followers better than they found them. They create and set TUFs and specific master the art of execution (MAX) acts that not only take people out of comfort zones, but also force an alternative approach to the business-as-usual mind-set to achieve them. In addition, they provide the training, empowerment, engagement, and accountability necessary to reach TUFs, especially as they map daily results on the MAX board and bring closure to each prior day's effort with an accountability-driven rhythm accountability meeting (RAM). When all is said and done, if you are not equipping and then stretching your people by creating a culture that fosters both a healthy discomfort and pressure to perform, then you are not leading them.

## The Front Line Determines the Bottom Line

2. *Managers lead from the rear; leaders from the front (the trenches).* Because they are enamored with *stuff*, leaders who overmanage become aloof and out of touch far more often than they engage in the trenches of their organization. In the trenches they could act as a catalyst, unleashing the full potential of their team. Instead they pencil-whip budgets and camp out on the cul-de-sac of counting beans, where they try to turn the numbers around. These managers ultimately fail to develop their most appreciable asset; talk like leaders but act like anchors.

   Conversely, leaders spend more time charting the course than they do charting the results. They focus on what is happening in the arena, as well as on what is on the horizon. This is because they know that the front line determines the bottom line. They just as quickly affirm good performances as they confront poor ones. These leaders have meaningful coaching, training, and mentoring time with their team; they engage with customers and proactively shape their culture rather than leaving it up for grabs. All this is to say: *They lead!*

### Change before You Have To!

3. *Managers resist change and defend the status quo; leaders rattle the status quo and change before they have to.* A key difference between the management and leadership mind-sets is that managers often wait for the bottom to fall out before they change, whereas leaders change before they have to. Managers who spend too little of their productive time with people, and too much of it with stuff, devolve into a defensive posture where they spend more time plugging holes, doing damage control, and reacting than they do leading. Because they are not in the trenches, or in touch with people to see and hear what is really going on in their organization, they are always too slow to change. Thus, they are more inclined to protect what is, than they are to rattle the status quo so that the organization can fight off complacency, make MAX adjustments through pruning, and continue to grow.

However, those leaders who stay in the trenches with their people see more clearly what needs to be changed and are quicker to take action. Too many leaders who were successful at one time because they led from the front and acted as change agents gradually withdraw from their catalyst role and begin presiding and administering as they roost in their office too often and for too long throughout the day. They regress in a way that takes them from risk taker, to caretaker, and ultimately to undertaker, as they preside over a lifeless enterprise that became comatose on their watch.

## Parting Thought

If you overmanage and underlead in areas such as the three I have presented, don't beat yourself up. After all, as I reminded you in the last chapter, we all get off track from time to time. What is important is that you become a more self-aware leader who is increasingly knowledge-able of his or her positive daily impact on others—or lack thereof—so that any temporary detour from strong leadership doesn't lead you into a dead end. If you would like regular tips on leadership to help keep you on track daily, follow me on Twitter @DaveAnderson100. *See? It's not rocket science!*

# CHAPTER 13

# You Are the Catalyst!

## The Challenge

For years, leadership pundits, authors, teachers, and experts have created complex and often too detailed job descriptions that confuse a leader as to what his or her ultimate role is within an organization. In the last chapter, I presented three areas where leaders tend to overmanage so that you may become more aware of when you're off track in vital leadership responsibilities. In the vein of keeping it simple (after all, it's not rocket science), I want to break those three roles down into one simple word that I believe may be the best one-word definition of a leader's role within an organization—catalyst.

## The Leader as a Catalyst!

The dictionary defines *catalyst* as "a person or thing that precipitates an event or change" (*Dictionary.com*, n.d.). Rarely does such an economy of words so accurately describe the expected role of a leader day in, day out. The bottom line is this: Leaders get paid to execute and to make things happen both personally and through each team member. No high-value leader goes to work each day to wait for something to happen, to watch it happen, or to wonder at day's end, "What happened?" Unfortunately, many low-value leaders routinely perform in this manner, by waiting until time is about to run out to find some heart, guts, or urgency or demonstrate true leadership (stretching, staying in the trenches, and changing before they have to). In fact, many organizations are burdened with at least one or two pretenders with titles, who we can only assume jumped into the leadership gene pool while the lifeguard wasn't looking. These cultural infections will eventually destroy your organization if you let them.

## Some Rocket Science Is Helpful

I apologize if you feel misled by my insertion of just a tad bit more rocket science. After all, this book's title implied that rocket science is not necessary to master the art of execution (MAX). However, in addition to the Second Law of Thermodynamics I introduced earlier, I'd like to add another law of physics that when understood and applied, can greatly aid us in our role to act as a daily catalyst.

**Sir Isaac Newton's First Law of Motion:** Objects in motion tend to stay in motion; objects at rest tend to stay at rest.

Considering this law, you can easily substitute the words *team members* for *objects* to see how this law is routinely lived out in an average organization on days when there is little structure, urgency, or accountability.

As a reminder, considering the Second Law of Thermodynamics, the leaders must assume the role of the "outside energy" necessary to cause activity, momentum, and results to wind up in an organization on the days when people are naturally inclined to wind down. Acting as this catalytic energy is natural once you install the MAX system within your culture. Every day energy is created when you increase focus on the ultimate few objectives (TUFs) and daily MAX acts, MAP your results on the MAX board, conduct daily rhythm of accountability meetings (RAMs), and continue to prune in pursuit of execution optimization. Remember, too, that every day means every day (EDMED)! Recalling the stretching, leading in the trenches, and changing before you have to strategies listed in the last chapter, consider weaving these two disciplines into your daily routine to infuse positive energy consistently:

1. *Conduct leadership wander-arounds periodically during the day.*
   Schedule time to put aside the paperwork and engage in people

work, by regularly getting in the trenches to observe, coach, support, ask questions, listen, give feedback, pat backs, provide corrective redirection, and engage team members and customers alike. You cannot expect to create energy and make positive things happen relying strictly on e-mails, texts or other technology.

2. *Schedule and consistently conduct one-on-one coaching sessions.* These developmental disciplines give you the chance to listen to, coach, reinforce, focus, and challenge each team member individually. One-on-ones should be scheduled on your calendar and conducted distraction-free. I provide an effective five-step process for conducting one-on-ones in my book *Up Your Business* (John Wiley & Sons 2007). You may also wish to take our online course for developing others, offered at www.learntolead.com.

## Five Key Questions

I will conclude with five quick questions to assess your effectiveness as a daily leadership catalyst in your organization:

- Daily, are you more prone to think, "What can I make happen for my team today?" or "I wonder what the team will do today"?
- What percentage of your day do you spend with *stuff* versus people?
- How much energy, urgency, and momentum exist in your organization early on in the month, quarter, year, or season, when there may not be as much pressure as when time is running out?
- Are you leaving your people better than you found them, and if so, how much of their growth can be attributed to your personal involvement as their leader and coach?
- If I joined your team today, could you show me the following in writing: your vision, mission, and core values; as well as my performance expectations daily, weekly, and monthly?

## Parting Thought

Any deficient answers to these questions can comprise your blueprint for stepping up your role as a daily leadership catalyst. *See? It's not rocket science*—okay, except for Newton's First Law of Motion and the Second Law of Thermodynamics.

# CHAPTER 14

# Buy-in Is Earned, Not Commanded!

## The Challenge

Although most leaders aren't foolish enough to say anything like the following aloud, they are prone to think it privately: "My people have to buy into me. I'm the boss; I own the place; my name is on the sign." These and other versions of positional leadership palavers demonstrate the debilitating duo of arrogance and ignorance. People *do not* have to buy into you or any other leader; they have the option to comply rather than commit. In other words, they have the choice to do just enough to get by and collect a paycheck, rather than stretch their efforts to second-mile performances. Buy-in must be earned; it cannot be assumed or commanded. Followers must buy into you in five key areas before they are eager to buy into the ultimate few objectives (TUFs) or into master the art of execution (MAX) as a process; I call these areas the five Cs. Frankly, if they are not buying into your aspirations, it is likely because they haven't bought into one or more of these aspects of you and your leadership. At least not yet.

## The Five Nonnegotiables of Buy-in

1. *Character:* Any follower, or potential follower for that matter, rightly asks the following about his or her leader: "Can I trust you?" Trust issues go beyond blatant offenses, such as lying, cheating, or stealing. It covers areas such as keeping commitments, leading by example, having a great work ethic, being teachable, giving away credit, admitting mistakes, and subordinating your own welfare to what's best for the team.

2. *Competence:* Any follower, or potential follower, rightly asks this question about his or her leader: "Do you know what you're doing?" People may like you, and you may have stellar character. But, if you're incompetent, they won't want to follow you. Followers want assurance that they're not going to get led into minefields and blown up because their leader is clueless or careless. They also want to believe they can learn, grow, and advance under your leadership watch. Top performers, especially, have little tolerance or respect for incompetent bosses who subject their teams to endless episodes of amateur hour.

3. *Consistency:* Any follower, or potential follower, rightly asks these questions about his or her leader: "Do you consistently demonstrate strong character, or do you bend it a bit when things get tough or to fit a budget? Do you demonstrate consistent competence, or just an occasional flash of brilliance?" Followers must believe their leader is consistently excellent in both the character and the competence arenas before they're anxious to follow the leader beyond baseline effort. With little consistency from the leader, there is little trust for the leader.

4. *Compassion:* Any follower, or potential follower, rightly asks this about his or her leader: "Do you really care about me, my welfare, and my future, or am I just another heifer in the herd?" You never have to answer this question verbally. Your attitude and actions—how much quality time you spend with them, for example—demonstrate it daily.

5. *Commitment:* Any follower, or potential follower, rightly asks this about his or her leader: "How committed are *you*? What price are you paying? Have you committed yourself to the cause, or are you

committing the cause to yourself?" Genuine commitment is not just declared. It is lived out daily in sacrificing for the team, making tough decisions, rattling the status quo, taking mature risks, accepting personal responsibility, and making necessary changes within yourself before trying to fix everyone else.

Other essential traits are important to followers, but most have their roots in one of these five Cs. Followers don't expect perfect leaders. They do, however, expect high levels of proficiency in all five of these areas. The great news is that once they believe in you, their attitudes and behaviors begin to change. They want to please you. They want to be part of your success. They want to be a part of what you're building and to share in your success. Sadly, it's possible to be in a leadership position for many years and still never earn buy-in into the five Cs. The results of failing to earn that buy-in include higher turnover, lower morale, and gross underachievement.

## Don't Forget the Newbies!

It's also important to recognize that you may have team members who've been with you for years and who fully buy into the five Cs of your leadership. But new hires aren't likely to jump automatically on the bandwagon. You cannot take these folks for granted. You will need to earn their buy-in as well. For instance, you will need to show them why MAX works and sell them on the process that others have long ago seen is great.

## Parting Thought

Buy-in does not normally happen overnight, but it will happen over time when you do your job. Buy-in is up to you. If you have the right people but they haven't bought into you, it's your fault. The good news is this means you can fix it. If you have been with your team a while and realize you haven't demonstrated the five Cs as you should have, it's not too late to earn their buy-in. Expect it to be harder, though. People will need to believe you have really changed and that your new character, competence, consistency, compassion, or commitment is not a fad or gimmick to trick them into improved performance. The five Cs are leadership basics, and much of what brings you success in your career will come from developing these five areas of personal development. Again, there are five key areas of buy-in, not 50, or even 15. *See? It's not rocket science!*

---

### Rocket Science Rant: Your Baggage Affects Everyone's Journey!

Throughout life, it is common for people to rush headlong toward a goal and once they get there, be at a loss for what to do next. Finishing school, getting married, or arriving at a vacation spot are examples of this. There is perhaps no more sought-after destination than becoming a leader where the "Now that I'm here what do I do?" anxiety takes hold. Yes, despite all the striving to rise through the ranks and get into leadership—arrive at a place—all too many people upon earning a leadership position fail to act as leaders. They ambitiously seek leadership but then fail to shift from position to performance and actually lead. This includes leaders in government, nonprofits, businesses, and more.

One reason why people in leadership positions don't lead effectively is because they never resist or shed the baggage that can come with leadership. It may sound odd to read that leadership comes with potential baggage, but it does—plenty of it. One's motives can become corrupt, insecurities can create anxiety, and you can become arrogant and full of yourself.

To convert *leadership* (as a position) to *lead* (as a performance), one must lose the *ership*. The *ership* is the baggage. Only after you have purged the baggage that comes with leadership can you lead effectively. If you consider the *ership* as an acronym, then the baggage one must lose to move from a position to performance looks like this:

- *Entitlement.* To lead effectively, a leader must focus less on what he or she is owed than on what he or she owes. He or she must prove himself or herself over again each day and not attempt to substitute tenure, experience, or credentials for results. Entitlement creates a *this company owes me/these people owe me* mind-set, which corrupts a leader and marginalizes the worth he or she brings to an organization. The bottom line is this: What you are ultimately entitled to as a leader is everything you have earned and deserve. Think you're owed more than that? Then there is a good chance you're a spoiled brat who needs to grow up. And it doesn't matter whether you're 60 years old—growing old and growing up are not synonymous.

- *Rights.* Immature leaders believe that leadership is about rights and perks rather than responsibilities and duty. However, to lead with integrity and inspire followers to reach essential TUFs, the leader must often subordinate his or her comfort and welfare to what is best for the team. Is this asking too much? Then get out of leadership! You're not a leader; you're a tyrant.

- *Selfishness.* To lead well, a leader must develop an abundance mind-set versus a scarcity mentality. He or she cannot afford to believe that if someone else gets something (a bigger budget, more resources, or greater responsibilities) that it means there is less for him or her. A secure leader avoids petty jealousies and turf wars because he or she understands that in a strong culture there will be just rewards for everyone doing an outstanding job. Leading unselfishly also means that the leader stops focusing solely on how far he or she goes or how much he or she gets personally and commits to bringing others across the finish line, too. Besides, as John C. Maxwell says, "If you're only in it for yourself, you're in a mighty small business." I would humbly add that you are also a narcissist.

- *Hypocrisy.* A credible leader leads with integrity. His or her words and deeds are consistent. He or she walks the talk, even when it is not easy, cheap, popular, or convenient. He or she is a living embodiment of company core values and would never ask someone else to do something he or she would not do personally. For instance, before credible leaders assign MAX acts for anyone else to execute daily, they have determined their own to achieve. They have their own personalized success profile (PSP) and expect the same accountability that the frontline people feel during a rhythm accountability meeting (RAM). Credible leaders also understand that
(*continued*)

(*continued*)

hypocrisy not only prevents buy-in but also destroys it if you happen to have duped others into buying into you in the first place.

- *Insecurity.* Astute leaders understand that the key to becoming more powerful is not through hoarding power and decision-making ability. The key is, however, for leaders to give it away to those in a better position to use it than they are. These secure leaders who do so are not threatened by ideas that oppose theirs or by people who are smarter or excel in areas of similar talents. Incidentally, if you think you are the only one on your team who can make a decision, have a good idea, or solve a problem, get over yourself. Everyone else already has.

- *Pride.* Pride is the number one cause of management failure, and an inflated ego is the largest obstacle to growing yourself or your team. To lead effectively, wise leaders cultivate humility. Only humble leaders see their role as one that finds ways to add value to and serves their team. Humble leaders seek out feedback, admit mistakes, give away credit, and shun the *been there, done that*, know-it-all arrogance prevalent in empty-suit leadership clowns.

To lead with integrity, those who find themselves in a leadership position must shed leadership's baggage, the *ership*. In doing so, they can lead with strength, and move miles ahead of those who either believe that a title makes them a leader or that they've been somehow made more competent because they were promoted. The leaders who give up baggage to grow up in leadership convert subordinates into followers, jobs into causes, and annual forecasts into compelling campaigns.

Entitlement, rights, selfishness, hypocrisy, insecurity, and pride—*ership*. Audit yourself and determine how much baggage is weighing down your ability to convert *passive* "leadership" into the *active* "lead." Then, resolve to give it up so that you and the team can continue to grow up. The sooner you do this, the better, because make no mistake about it; your leadership baggage affects everyone's journey. For some of you it's time to stop making everyone else's life miserable, get off the pedestal you have put yourself on, and ditch the excess baggage. The best leaders travel light.

# CHAPTER 15

# Get Your *Red* *Belt* On!

## The Challenge

Many leaders cannot survive success. Prosperity drains both their urgency and their drive, causing them to become complacent and turn into know-it-alls. As a result, hordes of successful leaders never come close to reaching their full potential. They dismiss a process like master the art of execution (MAX) because they are of the mind-set that says, "Look how well we've done without it; let's not rock the boat." They fail to understand that they have done well *despite* the fact they don't execute optimally, not *because* they don't execute optimally.

## The Red Belt Mind-Set

I learned about the red belt mind-set early in my study of the martial arts. My seven-time world champion instructor, Johnny Gyro, pointed to a wall with 12 belts displayed in order from white to black—the sequence of ranks I'd need to progress to become a black belt in the Tang Soo Do style of karate. He told me that red belts, the belt just before black, were the most dangerous fighters in the dojo. He explained that a common tendency of new first-degree black belts after passing their test was to put on weight because they would stop training as hard. Even though there are many degrees of black beyond the first, they would often turn into know-it-alls and spend more time giving advice than training to improve. The red belts, on the other hand, were still hungry. They were humble, were teachable, and had something to prove. He told me that over the years he had seen more *hungry* red belts knock down or knock out *complacent* black belts than he could count. Then he gave me this incredible advice: "If you ever become a black belt, continue to think like a red; act like a challenger even if you're the champ. Challengers are hungry, humble, and teachable; champs can become cocky, complacent, and lose their edge."

Although the martial arts application of a red belt mind-set was easy enough to understand, I also saw the business parallel: A company that has a record year, or rises to number one in a given area, earns its business equivalent of a black belt only to have the same kind of complacency set in. I wrote a well-publicized magazine article on the topic, and created a perennial best-selling product for our own business, marketing special red belts to organizations for display in their offices and conference rooms. These served as a reminder to everyone on the team that yesterday ended last night and that the team needed to prove themselves over again every day—that they needed to continue to act like a challenger with a red belt's mind-set.

## Hunger Must Start at the Top

You will not get the leaders right in your organization until they demonstrate red belt hunger. But here's the catch. You cannot make anyone hungry, nor can another person make you hungry. Hunger is an inside job. It's provoked from within by your personal *why*—your big, bold, compelling reasons for doing what you do. Leaders lose their way when they lose their why. In addition, followers working under a hunger-less leader have little chance of reaching their potential. I have seen it happen all too often over the decades. If a leader lets up in moderation, the followers let up in excess. The speed of the leader truly is the speed of the pack.

## Are You a Challenger or a Champ?

Following are 10 common contrasts between a challenger's (red belt) and a champion's (black belt) mind-set. Although there are always exceptions to these examples, the rule normally prevails. How would others who know your work habits best rate you in these areas?

- Challenger's mind-set: hungry. Champion's mind-set: satisfied.
- Challenger's mind-set: humble. Champion's mind-set: arrogant.
- Challenger's mind-set: teachable. Champion's mind-set: know-it-all.
- Challenger's mind-set: something to prove. Champion's mind-set: "been there, done that."
- Challenger's mind-set: willing to serve. Champion's mind-set: wants to be served.
- Challenger's mind-set: tries something new. Champion's mind-set: stuck in his or her ways.
- Challenger's mind-set: works with a sense of urgency. Champion's mind-set: paces himself or herself.
- Challenger's mind-set: plays to win. Champion's mind-set: plays not to lose.
- Challenger's mind-set: rattles the status quo. Champion's mind-set: defends the status quo.
- Challenger's mind-set: lives for the present and future. Champion's mind-set: lives in the past.

There are other differences, but these 10 paint a telling picture of why a leader wanting to get the culture right, get the team right, and master the art of execution must have a challenger's mind-set to succeed.

Here are five suggestions for developing a challenger's (a red belt's) state of mind. Use them to shape your personal leadership philosophy so that you can positively influence those you work with:

1. *Accept the fact that you are never as good as you think you are.* When you focus less on how successful you are, and more on closing the gap between your current status and your fullest potential, you will create a positive tension that keeps you both humble and hungry.

2. *When you're doing well, don't sit on the ball; run up the score.* Never settle for your fair share of the market. Strive for an unfair share. Don't make it a goal to create a level playing field in your market area. Instead, work hard to make the playing field so unlevel that your organization has an insanely unfair advantage over your competition. If you're not thinking in these terms, you've probably already regressed from high gear into neutral. All that's missing from your office is the hammock, a pitcher of margaritas, and a Panama hat.

3. *Embrace* urgency *as a core value. Urgency* is one of LearnToLead's five corporate core values, as well as one of my personal values. You must convince yourself that there is power in *now*, not later. You may never get later. Act *now*!

4. *Be an* and then some *leader.* Do what is expected *and then some*. Pay the price *and then some*. Keep your commitments *and then some*.

5. *Hunger sustains MAX.* Without a red belt mind-set the ultimate few objectives (TUFs) will be too safe, and your rhythm of accountability meetings (RAMs) inconsistent, because your allegiance to the status quo will sideline your desire to reach for the stars.

## Parting Thought

Be an example for your team, and work with the hunger, discipline, humility, intensity, and teachability of a red belt. Set your goal to reach the top, but don't stop once you become a grand master. Maintain the mind-set of a challenger. Master Gyro gave me this great advice years later during my own black belt ceremony: "You worked hard and deserve this. But what this really means is that now you're an advanced beginner; there's still a lot to learn." Redefine your whys. Make them more compelling than ever before. Then, implement MAX into your culture, and work harder on your culture and team than ever before. But remember that it all really begins with one simple decision to start by working harder yourself. *See? It's not rocket science!* (To order your own special Stay Hungry Red Belts for you and your team, visit our store at www.learntolead.com.)

# 16

# The Truth about Mediocrity

## The Challenge

Mediocrity is both dangerously and subtly seductive. *Mediocre* is defined as "of only ordinary or moderate quality; neither good nor bad; barely adequate" (*Dictionary.com*, n.d.). Essentially, mediocrity is the opposite of excellent, which is synonymous with being superior. Without red belt hunger, you spend more time working around mediocrity than you do dealing with it. Consequently, you allow that which is average, ordinary, and not outstanding to linger within your organization. Because you learn to live with mediocrity, you are prone to permit it to endure even longer. Therein lies its seductive danger: The longer you live *with* mediocrity, the longer you live *in* mediocrity. No matter what aspect of your organization is mediocre, be it a strategy, policy, process, practice, or person, it will eventually infect your culture and seriously debilitate your ability to execute and achieve meaningful results. To fully implement and sustain master the art of execution (MAX), there must come a time when you get the pruning shears out and devastate mediocrity (both personal and organizational) rather than defend it, rationalize it, minimize it, externalize it, trivialize it, or compromise with it.

## Take Responsibility for What's Mediocre in Your Organization

A clear sign of leadership maturity is the willingness to take responsibility. One aspect of this virtue is refusing to make excuses for personal failures or for the failure of others. Frankly, listening to others blame is one of my pet peeves. Little rubs me rawer than when someone attempts to defend failed actions or inferior results by sanitizing the fact that their past decisions to settle have caught up with them and are now costing them results. I am also convinced that excuses are the DNA of underachievers; they mark *you* as average, ordinary, and not outstanding. Good luck trying to earn buy-in, build trust, stay hungry, or implement MAX effectively when you're known as a defender of mediocrity—an aider and abettor of failed potential.

Here are five thoughts concerning mediocrity to help you or someone you care about right the course and stay on a path of personal responsibility. This path will elevate self-worth, as well as the value you bring to others and to your organization.

## Five Truths about Mediocrity

1. *Mediocrity begins with* me. It is not something that an outside force does to you. No one is born mediocre; mediocrity is a choice. In fact, it is a result of the choices you have made, the conditions you have accepted, or the wrong actions you have taken during your career and life. Before you can hope to get your culture right, your team right, or the MAX process right, you've got to purge what's mediocre from your attitude, leadership philosophy, daily routine, and skill set. Furthermore, if you have little or no talent for what you're doing, and are mediocre as a result, you can still choose to go do something you're suited for and not settle for mediocrity. Again, *spending your life mired in mediocrity is a choice!*

2. *Mediocrity is a personal concession to do less than your best.* What the mediocre are really saying is, "This is good enough, so deal with it." When you substitute compromises for excellence, you make the *good enough* concession and resign yourself to living out a career and life that are average, ordinary, and not outstanding, rather than the best they can be. (You may as well have your heirs put a big 0 on your tombstone while you're at it.)

3. *You break free from mediocrity by making better decisions, not by waiting for favorable conditions.* This should encourage you, because while you cannot control conditions, you do have control over your decisions. You can't choose what happens around you, but you can control the decisions within you.

4. *Living in denial prolongs your marriage to mediocrity.* Denial is defined as "disbelief in the existence or reality of a thing" (*Dictionary.com*, n.d.). Thus, if you don't face it, you cannot fix it. If you won't acknowledge it, you will never change it. The box of mediocrity you have put yourself in will one day become a casket. If you are settling for mediocrity, it is time to stop dog paddling as you tread water and start rocking the boat.

5. *Make your break with any mediocre aspect of your life by deciding to do the following:*

   a. Put away your tendency to blame, get your *red belt* on, and accept responsibility for your results. Understand that one of the best days of your life is the day that you renounce compromises to your potential, get serious, and become a man or woman of excellence.

   b. Commit to personal development so that you elevate the quality of your thinking and are able to make better personal decisions concerning your own attitude, character choices, application of knowledge, and strengthening of discipline.

   c. Get clearer about what you want, and then resolve to pay the price to achieve it. Decide up front to ditch the costly cop-outs that keep you from life's best, and hold yourself accountable for expecting and accepting only what is excellent.

   d. Determine right now what is average, ordinary, or not out-standing in your daily routine, personal habits or performance, relationships, culture, team, policies, practices, processes, strategies, et cetera. Upon doing this, redefine what excellence should look like in those areas, and realign, revitalize, or remove what's necessary to achieve that end.

## Parting Thought

One of the saddest legacies for many who choose to lead mediocre lives will be that when they die, it will be as though they never lived. But what's sadder yet is that when the sweat of their deathbed wakes them up to the fact that they have missed their life and that it's too late, the classic lament of the mediocre will haunt them: "I could have. I should have. If only I would have." Each day you really have only two choices: performance or excuses. Choose well because the result becomes your life and your legacy. Two choices. *See? It's not rocket science!*

# CHAPTER 17

# Beware the Five Seductions of Leadership

## The Challenge

Your number one vulnerability as a leader is the one you are unaware of. It is the threat you don't know exists and never see coming. It is the unexpected sucker punch that has the potential to set you back, sometimes to an irrecoverable level. This section will help you cope with this challenge by shining a spotlight on five of these clear and present dangers to your leadership.

## Watch Out Fors and To Dos

Up to this point in the second strategy for mastering the art of execution (MAX), "Get the Leaders Right!," we've discussed these key points:

- Don't overmanage and underlead.
- Stretch, lead from the trenches, and change before you have to.

- Your role as a daily catalyst.
- Earn buy-in with the five Cs.
- Shed the baggage that affects everyone else's journey.
- The importance of staying hungry with a red belt mind-set.
- The truth about mediocrity—it starts with *me*.

These chapters have blended *what to watch out fors* along with *to dos*. This chapter adds to the *what to watch out for* column.


## The Truth about Seduction

*Seduce* is defined as "to lead astray, as from duty, rectitude, or the like; corrupt" (*Dictionary.com*, n.d.). Other people, emergencies, and conditions of all sorts arise as daily seducers that can deepen a leader's fray. Becoming aware of these seducers is the first stop to identifying them, overcoming them, or avoiding them altogether. In doing this, you can allow yourself and others to execute daily MAX acts, as well as install and facilitate MAX throughout your organization.

Leadership seductions are subtle. They normally lull you, rather than knock you, off course. They inflict daily what the poet David Whyte (1996) wrote: "I turned my head for a moment and it became my life." As a result, leadership seductions cause you to work longer and harder to achieve your TUFs, because you spend a lot of time being chased by what's urgent. Likewise, you find yourself majoring in minor things rather than executing, holding daily rhythm accountability meetings (RAMs), or engaging in necessary pruning disciplines. Oftentimes, you don't even notice this has happened until it is too late. A book section for getting the leaders right would not be complete without studying leadership seductions, because they are facts of life and all leaders are challenged by them eventually.

Although the following list of leadership seductions is nowhere near complete, the five seductions I present are devastating in their ability to prevent you from leading at your highest potential. It's important that you not only face them but continually work to prune them from your life as well.

## *Seduction 1—Leaders Are Seduced by Motion*

Back in Part One, "Get the Process Right!," I cautioned you against mistaking motion for progress. Here we will expand on the issue. This seduction actually has two applications. The first concerns your approach to daily job duties. When seduced by motion, you can find yourself immersed in such a frantic swirl of daily motion that you routinely confuse activity with accomplishment, put second things first, do the wrong things often and well, and achieve little meaningful results by day's end.

The following questions help diagnose your vulnerability to being seduced by motion:

- Do you schedule MAX acts and work the rest of the day around them, or do you try to cram your MAX acts into a fray-dominated day?
- Do you feel a false sense of accomplishment because you've been busy and in motion all day, or do you rate your effectiveness by whether you spend enough time on the right things? What does your personal MAX board reflect in this regard?
- When you disengage from the essential and immerse in the trivial, how quickly do you catch yourself and correct your course?

The second application of seduction by motion concerns your team's daily activities. Consider these questions:

- As you survey your team, are you at ease because everyone appears busy, or do you dig deeper to determine whether they are actually executing what their personalized success profiles (PSPs) prescribe? In other words, are you prone to confuse their doing a lot with doing what matters?
- Are RAMs held daily and without fail to reinforce the importance of executing high-leverage tasks daily and hold each team member accountable for doing so?

*Remedy*—*Measure your personal and team's effectiveness by what you put into the hours, instead of the number of hours you put in.* Resolve not to confuse motion with progress. Remember that nothing tells the story of your success, or failure, faster in this regard than the condition of your MAX board.

## Seduction 2—Leaders Are Seduced by Tradition

This seduction includes the tendency to bond with, and become desensitized to the mediocrity of some tenured employees, your old ways of doing things, and key elements of the status quo. Frankly, it's far easier to ignore the necessity of pruning. It is simpler instead to defend the status quo, "how we've always done things," as well as nonperforming employees when things are going well. But to ward off the complacency that will break your momentum, you must continue to challenge and attack the status quo before the bottom falls out and you fall into a rut. Unfortunately, it often takes a crisis to shake an organization out of its immersion in, and addiction to, tradition.

*Remedy—Practice the discipline of changing before you have to and renewing yourself in the absence of a crisis.* Teach and expect your people to do likewise. Internalize the discipline of consistent pruning to realign, revitalize, or remove what's inhibiting execution excellence.

## Seduction 3—Leaders Are Seduced by Tolerance

Hollywood, the media, and political correctness will wrongly convince you that you should tolerate just about anything today and that not doing so makes you hateful or harsh.

However, the presence of absolutes and what you refuse to tolerate largely define both your culture and your personal leadership. In a strong culture there still is right and wrong, winning and losing, and success and failure, as well as consequences that accompany bad behavior and poor performance.

*Remedy—Find and eliminate gray areas for performance and behavior shortfalls with clearer expectations and consequences for failure.* Be specific and follow through. MAX boards and daily RAMs are key allies in this regard.

## Seduction 4—Leaders Are Seduced by Stupidity

Ignorance means you do not know better. To be stupid means you know better but do the wrong thing anyway. Incidentally, moronic means notably stupid, indicating perhaps that stupidity has become a lifestyle (in which case it's certainly best to stop at stupid). The problem is that stupidity is often masked, and leaders are seduced by it when they are successful despite themselves.

It's essential to face reality and understand that if you do stupid things and are successful, your success is not *because* you do stupid things, but *despite* the fact you do stupid things. You can rest assured that eventually, *stupidity* will catch up with you.

*Remedy—Look at areas where you know personal and team behaviors fall short of excellent and where you have felt no urgency to correct them because poor results have not yet reached crisis levels.* Then, quickly shake off the seduction of stupidity by deciding to do what you know is beneficial in the long term. Be aware that the shelf life for getting away with stupidity in the short term may be nearing its expiration date.

### Seduction 5 — Leaders Are Seduced by Success

Remember the lesson of the red belt mind-set: Success is an intoxicant, and intoxicated people don't behave rationally. Because of this, success lies at the core of the other four seductions. Success can make people so arrogant, prideful, and blind to reality that they keep skipping right down the yellow brick road until they smack right into a wall of irrelevance.

*Remedy—Understand Jim Collins's principle that "the enemy of great is good"* (n.d.). This simply means that the number one reason why so many reading these words are unlikely to become great is because they have gotten good. As a result, they have lost their killer instinct and have stopped stretching, changing, risking, holding others accountable, and narrowing their focus. This doesn't have to happen on your leadership watch, and it will not if you install and execute MAX and apply the *to dos* and heed the *watch out fors* listed throughout this chapter.

### Parting Thought

Motion, tradition, tolerance, stupidity, and success—all simple words that pack a low blow to your leadership when they become seductions that blur your focus or drain your drive. They're not complex concepts.

We understand what they are, what they can do, and now how to prevent their impact. The key is becoming more aware that they exist and resolving to stay on track with your daily leadership behaviors as you work daily to master the art of execution. And every day means every day. *See? It's not rocket science!*

# 18

# Five Ways Conventional Wisdom Destroys Your Potential

## The Challenge

An abundance of simpleminded leaders routinely follow the what's *conventional* herd rather than challenging what's always been or the conventional wisdom that sounds good but has serious flaws. If you are going to get the process, leaders, culture, and team right, it's important to remember this: For the most part, the herd is average; when you follow it, you tend to step in what it leaves behind.

## If You Want to Change Your Results, Change Your Philosophy

Your personal and business philosophies go a long way in determining whether you can even begin to approach reaching your fullest potential as a leader. Because your thoughts determine behaviors, and your behaviors determine results, it's essential to examine the leadership philosophy at the core of your results.

Following are five conventional yet failed philosophies that leaders often embrace, costing them and their organizations dearly in terms of results. Unfortunately, some of these beliefs are so commonly stated that they have become accepted as absolutes.

1. *"Everyone has unlimited potential."* This is true. Everyone has unlimited potential at *something*. No one has unlimited potential at *everything*. People have unlimited potential only in an area where they are gifted or where they possess talent. The problem is that leaders routinely invest more time, money, and training in people who have no talent for what they're being paid to do. Their belief that "everyone has unlimited potential" dupes them into thinking that with enough time and investment, they can make the untalented excellent. The truth is, the best leaders can hope to do is make them less bad.

2. *"The more tasks you can do, the more valuable you are to the organization."* It is ironic how many times people will boast of being a jack of all trades. No one ever brags about the latter half of that cliché and declares, "I'm a master of nothing," which is the common result of celebrating the former.

   We all have a zone, which is our area of giftedness, where we're at our best, and where we bring the greatest value to the organization. Every time you leave your zone, you lose some of your effectiveness. Get out of it too often, or stay out of it for too long, and you can lose your relevance as a leader and your passion for what you do. It can also cause you to micromanage as you meddle in areas where you have little expertise. Although it is healthy to know a little about a lot of things to improve your perspective, it is not wise to do a little of a lot of things because you'll be out of your zone a lot. To get in your zone and stay there as often as possible, it's wise to follow the late Stephen Covey's advice: "The job of a leader is to build a complementary team where every strength is made effective and each weakness is made irrelevant" (quoted in Maxwell 2013). This happens when people are allowed to stay in their zone and maximize their strengths. In addition, it occurs when you have people on your team who are good at the things you are not good at, creating a healthy and complementary team balance.

3. *"To be fair, I need to give everyone equal time, attention, and opportunities."* In today's politically correct, hypersensitive, *everyone gets a trophy* culture, it is easy to get caught up in this ridiculous and destructive thought. Without question, effective leaders must be fair. But fairness doesn't mean sameness; fairness means justice, and justice means people get what they earn and deserve based on past performance. It's probably safe to say that based on their past performance, not all members of a team deserve the same amount of your time, opportunities, pay plan, attention, discretion, and the like. In fact, it's unfair to withhold these things from someone who has earned them and give them to a team member who has not.

4. *"It's never good to quit."* You should not quit if the reason you're quitting is because something is hard, makes you uncomfortable, or is painful. Those situations build character and help you grow. However, if people or things are not improving, regardless of how much effort you or they pour into them (because they have no aptitude for it), then they are probably wise to quit it and go find their thing. A foolish consistency, invested into efforts that bring little or no return, will deplete an organization's morale, momentum, and financial resources.

5. *"I don't want to make people uncomfortable."* Here's the problem with that failed philosophy: It is nearly impossible to learn, grow, or progress consistently when you are comfortable. In fact, most changes will always create some degree of pain and discomfort, but that is a positive occurrence because both are signs of growth (that's why they're called *growing pains* and not *growing comforts*). Leadership is about bringing people through the pain and discomfort necessary to get to the next level and teaching them that there isn't a prize without paying a price. If you never make your people uncomfortable by stretching their abilities, you are doing them a terrible disservice.

## Parting Thought

Keep this in mind: Your results will not improve until the behaviors do. Similarly, behaviors won't change until your philosophy improves. In other words, the core issue isn't what's going on between your walls but between your ears. *See? It's not rocket science!*

### Rocket Science Rant: The Lost Art of Taking Personal Responsibility!

For the past two decades, I've written and spoken extensively about topics such as discipline, accountability, and focusing on what you *can* control in your life and business. These are principles I have personally embraced, and they have proved themselves effective in my own life.

In the late 1970s and early 1980s, I worked in my parents' restaurant business that eventually failed. Suddenly, I was unemployed. The economy was mired in 21 percent interest rates, 13 percent inflation, and 11 percent unemployment. The conventional excuse was, "You can't find a job in this economy." I found three. My red belt hunger—my *why*—was triggered by the fact I was living in a rat-infested house with no furniture, and my food supply consisted mostly of refried beans and tortillas. Granted, the jobs I had weren't what I really wanted, nor were they what I thought I was qualified for. But, they were what was available, so I was grateful to have them. I sold products door-to-door for two companies and then delivered corn tortillas to restaurants in the evenings for 50 cents per case.

A few years later, while living with my wife and daughter in the ugliest trailer, in the ugliest trailer park in town, I switched from selling insurance to selling cars. In seven years I worked my way from being a salesperson in Texas to the number two man in a 300-million-dollar dealership group in California. When new owners unceremoniously forced me out, I didn't sue, protest, or *occupy* the dealerships; I, with my wife, founded our company, LearnToLead (which, by God's grace, has grown substantially and prospers to this day).

When six dozen publishers turned down my book ideas for *Selling above the Crowd* and *No-Nonsense Leadership*, I exerted the effort and expense to self-publish, distribute, and publicize them. Their ensuing success attracted John Wiley & Sons, the world's largest business book publisher, into my life, and we have now published 11 books together. My hard-knocks first publishing experience has reaffirmed my belief that if something is important to you, you will find a way. If it isn't, you will find an excuse.

I don't share these incidents to try to impress you but to impress upon you that I have been broke, been at the bottom, and been the chief architect behind numerous failed ideas and ventures. But upon hitting the wall, I chose to bounce rather than splatter. As a result, I can assail today's growing *victim* culture with a clear conscience and credibility, because like many of you, when I found myself in a crisis, I didn't try to whine my way out. I didn't wish my way out, wait my way out, or demand a handout. I got off my rear end and worked my way out.

### It's All about You

Just so we're clear about the importance of taking personal responsibility, quickly consider the following points in relation to just one aspect of your organization: master the art of execution (MAX).

- If you choose the wrong ultimate few objectives (TUFs), you're to blame.
- If you choose the wrong MAX acts, it's your fault.
- If your MAX board isn't kept up-to-date, that's on you.
- If you don't hold rhythm of accountability meetings (RAMs), look in the mirror.
- If you fail by not continually pruning to optimize all aspects of your organization, you're responsible for that failure.

Get the idea? This *really* isn't rocket science.

### Success—or the Lack of It—Is about Choices

When you choose to not take personal responsibility for your results, or for your life, you choose instead to become a victim. You choose to slouch through life, assume that position, and

*(continued)*

(*continued*)

complain to all who will listen that life isn't doing enough to make you happy. This sort of behavior is especially disturbing in supposedly mature adults, but it's absolutely abominable in leadership, where more is expected from those who have been given much. If blaming and making excuses, rather than taking responsibility, has become a personal tendency, then perhaps the following points will shake you out of denial and purge a few "it's not my fault" fantasies from your vocabulary. Pay attention: The parts that make you the most uncomfortable may have the most to teach you.

- Becoming *is more important than* getting. Until you choose to become more than you are in areas such as attitude, discipline, your philosophy, and skill development, you are unlikely to get much more than you've got. When you get more (usually because it is given to you) without becoming more, you rarely get to keep it for long and won't have the skills to replace it. If you are not being paid what you need, then becoming more is a far more effective strategy than demanding more. You cannot expect to demand your way or protest your way to greatness. If you're not becoming more, it is because you have chosen not to. You are not a victim.

- *Attitude is a choice.* You may not be able to choose what happens to you, but you can choose your response to it. The quality of your response will greatly determine the quality of your job, bank balance, relationships, and life. If you have a lousy attitude, it's because you choose a lousy attitude. Nobody did it to you, so suck it up, grow up, and step up. You are not a victim.

- *Discipline is a choice.* No one is born disciplined or not. Discipline develops when you get clear about what you want, decide to pay the price necessary to get it, and resolve to give up what hinders your quest. If you are undisciplined, it's not because you were born that way; it's because you've chosen to go through life seeking prizes without paying prices. Quit sniveling while you look for free lunches and step up. You are not a victim.

- *Character is a choice.* Character is the combination of moral and ethical qualities that you have decided to embrace and apply in your life. If you lack strong character, you can't blame Mom and Dad, the government, or your teachers. Ultimately, you get to choose what's important to you and what's not. Your character will develop—or not—in accordance with those convictions. If you have weak character, then stop faulting conditions and blame your lousy decisions. You are not a victim.

- *Failure is not an accident.* Anyone can catch a good or bad break from time to time, but over the course of a career or a lifetime, you don't accidentally fail or succeed. Stop resenting other people because of their good luck, and stop blaming bad luck for your lack of success. To help you out, digest this reality tidbit: Bad luck is the perfume of choice that losers spray to disguise the stench of their poor decisions, absent discipline, and anemic work ethic. You are not a victim!

## Parting Thought

Taking personal responsibility for your results and your life is so rare today that it's a sure way to stand out. In fact, you should be strongly encouraged by the fact that it's not crowded at the top; it's crowded at the bottom. There is intense competition among the mediocre hordes who go through life belching out the baloney for why they never brought home the bacon.

# CHAPTER 19

# The Power of Preparation

## The Challenge

Many leaders are good at winging it, shooting from the hip, or operating out of instinct every day and still getting results. They have high talent and energy levels that allow them to move forward despite their lack of adequate preparation or personal growth. Eventually, however, this person plateaus and soon discovers that he or she failed to lay a sound foundation to sustain and increase that success. They've taken the organization as high as they could employing the sloppy strategy of making things up as they went along.

## Power Points on Preparation

Preparation builds confidence, reduces stress, and helps you move your organization ahead further and faster. Knowing in advance what to do as you face certain scenarios defines your leadership as strong, assured, and decisive. Following are 14 common realities that we all face as leaders. Your proper response to them will help shape your process, culture, team, and results.

1. *The prepared response for winning is to:* give credit to the team and then spend 80 percent of your time building on your strengths and 20 percent fixing weaknesses. Working on weaknesses gets you by; working on strengths gets you great.

2. *The prepared response for losing is to:* accept responsibility for the failure, make or accept no excuses, learn from it, adjust, and grow because of it.

3. *The prepared response for making a mistake is to:* admit it quickly, learn from it, and don't repeat it.

4. *The prepared response for a team member's mistake is to:* point it out quickly, and in your critique, separate the performer from the performance. Use the error as a teaching tool, not as a battering ram. Redefine your expectation as well as what good performance looks like. Then insist the team member take another shot.

5. *The prepared response for feedback, positive or negative, is to:* say, "Thank you." Don't allow praise to inflate your ego. Nor should you permit your ego to dismiss valid observations about how you can improve your leadership and performance.

6. *The prepared response for a customer complaint is to:* treat it as a gift and seize the opportunity to convert a disappointed customer into an enthusiastic member of your unpaid sales force. Wow him or her with your eagerness and ability to make things right without making hoops to jump through, a blame game, or delays.

7. *The prepared response for relational conflict between you and another team member is to:* make the first move humbly to address the issue, admit any wrongdoing, flush out and deal with hard feelings, gain closure, and move forward in unity. Throughout the process, remember that in most cases, it's far more productive that your need to be right is subordinate to the long-term vitality of the relationship's health.

8. *The prepared response for a strategic plan that isn't working is to:* change it. Remain locked like a laser beam on the ultimate few objectives (TUFs) without becoming attached to how you will get there. Reevaluate master the art of execution (MAX) acts, and make sure they are the most high-leverage tasks. As you

move forward, remain focused on results yet flexible in your approach to securing them.

9. *The prepared response for feeling stuck, burned out, or void of passion for your work is to:* read a book, attend a course, engage, and pick the brains of those more successful than you in a given area. Learning is energizing and has a catalytic ability to dislodge you from ruts. The better you get on the job, the less time you have to spend there, and the more time you can spend away from it, pursuing balance in other areas of your life that contribute to your overall well-being.

10. *The prepared response for realizing that your culture has become weak with accountability is to:* destroy gray areas by redefining performance and behavioral expectations for both daily activities and monthly results. Put them in writing, offer fast feedback on performance to keep people on the right track, and apply consequences for failure when necessary. Pay particular attention to the next section of this book, "Get the Culture Right!"

11. *The prepared response for a growing sense of entitlement among employees is to:* carefully read and apply the strategies that address this in "Get the Culture Right!"

12. *The prepared response for an employee who blames and fails to take responsibility for his or her results is to:* turn his or her head away from the *blame conditions* window and into the mirror of personal responsibility. Help the employee face and focus on the aspects of his or her job that he or she can control. This includes but is not limited to attitude, discipline, and character choices; where they spend their time and with whom they spend it; the choice to grow, follow up, and hold others accountable; following prescribed processes; deciding who joins the team and who must leave it; and many more.

13. *The prepared response for an employee who offers excuses for task failure is to:* teach him or her that you will accept explanations, not excuses, for task failure. Explanations relate what went wrong, or didn't get done, along with the acceptance of personal responsibility for the failure and a plan for how to succeed next time. Excuses simply blame. *Special note:* Lest you become a

hypocrite, if you are going to stop accepting excuses, you must first renounce them personally.

14. *The prepared response for realizing your team is in more of a maintenance than a stretch mode is to:* acknowledge your role in allowing stagnation to grip the culture because you've failed to stretch, change, lead from the trenches, and act as a daily catalyst. Then redefine expectations, and begin leading again—daily. Every day means every day!

## Parting Thought

It's not normally a seismic shift in marketplace, economic, or political conditions that can set back your leadership progress and impair results. It is the simple, common occurrences such as the 14 listed, that when faced by the unprepared, can unnecessarily derail momentum, morale, and personal credibility. The more you prepare for these certainties, the less you will have to repair because you weren't ready. *See? It's not rocket science!*

# CHAPTER 20

# A Blueprint for Making the Tough Calls

## The Challenge

In visiting with thousands of leaders in dozens of industries over the past two decades, one thing is clear: The people who are expected to make fast and tough decisions are rarely trained how to do so. As a result, they wrongly make costly gut decisions, or indecision prevails in areas that end up costing the organization plenty. Although there is not a one-size-fits-all mechanism for making tough decisions, attendees to my workshops have found it useful when I present a series of filters to help them assess tough situations realistically and make the tough calls necessary for the organization to move forward faster.

## Three Key Filters to Improve Your Decision Making

Although there is not space for all the decision-making scenarios I generally provide in a seminar setting, the following three filters have wide applicability and should help you to reassess and act immediately on areas you've been pondering. Some of these filters apply strictly to personnel assessment, and others address strategies, policies, and more.

### The Hope versus Wish Filter: Are You Hoping or Wishing for Improvement?

Wondering just how much longer to work with an underperforming person, strategy, policy, vendor, and the like can immobilize you. This filter may help clear it up for you.

*Hope* is defined as "grounds for believing something in the future will occur" (*Dictionary.com*, n.d.). In other words, you could take the case to court and win based on evidence that things are headed in the right direction. . . . *Ladies and gentlemen of the jury, here are my grounds for believing this underperformer is on the right track and will become a success with our company: He has developed this productive habit, broken this unproductive habit, made the following positive attitude adjustment, developed this new skill, and improved these two current skills, and his performance during the past three months, although only marginally better, is headed in the right direction.*

Without grounds for believing—specific evidence like that presented—you're not hoping; you're wishing. Wishing is an unacceptable strategy for growing your organization.

So that you may appreciate the contrast between genuine hope and foolish wishes, consider the definition of *wish*: "a strong desire for something to occur that probably will not happen" (*Dictionary.com*, n.d.). Obviously, the key difference between hoping and wishing is the all-important "grounds for believing."

You can use the same hope versus wish filter to assess marketing messages and media, hiring and training strategies, and the list goes on. Consider a decision that you have been stuck on. Other than the fact you want it to work out, what grounds do you have for believing that tomorrow will be any different from today?

Understanding the difference between hoping and wishing will especially be helpful as you decide which category of pruning is necessary for less-than-optimal processes, policies, strategies, expenditures, vendors, and people. You can realign and revitalize areas where there is hope, but in cases where you're simply wishing, they must be removed.

## The Advocate, Apathetic, or Saboteur Filter

When you present a change to your team—a new ultimate objective (TUF), master the art of execution (MAX) act, policy, strategy, pay plan, or work schedule—not everyone will respond the same way. It is important to have a filter to discern the three primary groups of people responding to change and devise a strategy for each.

1. *Advocates.* This group favors the change and will speak well of both it and you. It is essential that you do all you can to make sure key influencers are in this group before you announce anything major to the group overall. If they are, you will have momentum and instant traction. If they are not, the change is dead on arrival.

2. *Apathetics.* This group is not as bad as it sounds. These folks won't do anything to derail or stall the change, but they will not do anything to help it either. The definition of *apathetic* is "not interested or concerned; indifferent or unresponsive" (*Dictionary .com*, n.d.). True to their name, these folks are apathetic, and sometimes they have reason to be. They've seen so many flavors of the month, so to speak, and management whims come and go in the past that they're content to sit on the sideline to see if this one is for real before becoming emotionally invested. Do your job, follow through, and the apathetics will come on board.

3. *Saboteurs.* These people are trouble and will try to derail your efforts overtly or covertly. Sometimes they do it in obvious ways by challenging you publicly. Other times they do it with more stealth by planting seeds of doubt and resistance in the meeting after the meeting you can expect them to conduct. Saboteurs are cancers and must be addressed quickly, privately, and firmly. If you cannot gain the agreement that they are on board, then you may have to let them go. This especially holds true if this is a major change. Otherwise they will manifest as cultural cancers that undermine team morale, momentum, efforts, and your personal credibility.

A potential fourth group that teeters somewhere between the others is the honest skeptics. These folks have legitimate questions, differences, or concerns they want cleared up before buying in and moving forward. This *does not* mean they are saboteurs. If you address their concerns effectively, and show what you're doing is effective and beneficial, you will win them over. If not, they can descend into the apathetic or saboteur ranks.

By understanding these groups, you can devise a strategy for each, and decide how best to implement the MAX process and other changes necessary, as you move toward achieving your organizational TUFs.

## The Three Ts Filter

An exercise I have taught for decades is rooted in zero-based thinking—determining that if you were to start over from zero, would you do what you are doing now. This works well when evaluating the performance of people on your team. Here's how. Go through each name on your team, and ask, "Knowing what I now know about 'Fred,' if he applied for the job today, would I hire him?" If the answer is yes, great; go to the next name. If the answer is some version of "Are you kidding me?," you can apply the three Ts filter:

- *Train.* This is the first and best option. If you do not believe he or she has had the training or coaching to succeed, do your job and fix this.
- *Transfer.* This is not an option for someone with unsatisfactory character, attitude, drive, or energy, because it's more likely he or she needs a change of self than a change of scene. It *is* an option for someone who is misemployed because he or she lacks the talent for a given position and would be better suited elsewhere.
- *Terminate.* If the first two options won't work, and you have already renounced the pervasive and costly fourth T—tolerate—it's time to move on.

Much like hoping versus wishing, the three Ts filter can help you when you are evaluating team members by determining the appropriate pruning strategy. The first two Ts would fall under the revitalize category—business as usual is not an option, so something must change. The third T qualifies for removal—the situation is beyond hope and must be terminated.

## Parting Thought

Assessing difficult situations and then acting on them with as much speed as you possibly can is essential for credible leadership and moving your organization forward. But, to do so, you must have filters like the three listed that help you quickly face reality about what you're really dealing with and determine which course of action is appropriate. With these simple filter tools at your disposal, you won't require hours of debate and death by meeting to know which course is the right one to take. *See? It's not rocket science!*

# CHAPTER 21

# Four Ways to Measure Your Leadership

## The Challenge

Ultimately, all leaders are measured by results. However, results alone can be a misleading indicator for how effective one is in his or her leadership role. Hot economies, popular products, weak competitors, or other favorable conditions can make the terrible appear tolerable, the subpar look good, and the good appear great.

To gain a more objective view of your own, and other leaders' true effectiveness, we will need to dig deeper and examine four key areas that serve as an acute and telling report card of true leadership abilities; all of which portend one's potential to execute effectively. Below are four quadrants of leadership that offer a more insightful view into your own leadership and that of others within your organization.

## The First Quadrant of a Leader's Report Card: The Culture You've Created

A leader is the chief architect and primary influencer of his or her culture. He or she can either shape it productively or have it destructively shaped by outside forces, such as indifference, an absence of absolutes, and entitlement. The next section, "Get the Culture Right!," will go into far greater detail in this regard. For now, because culture is palpable (you tend to feel it even more than you see it), evaluate the following criteria for measuring the culture you're responsible for:

- Clear and high-performance expectations in writing for daily, weekly, and monthly activities and outcomes—master the art of execution (MAX) acts and the ultimate few objectives (TUFs).
- Very little gray area.
- Very little entitlement.
- Very little, if any, deadweight.
- Swift and firm accountability.
- A strong team-first concept.
- Strong peer pressure to perform.
- High morale.
- Great customer experiences resulting in outstanding customer retention.
- A *second mile is standard* work ethic.
- Leadership acts as a catalyst and is engaged daily in the trenches.

As you might have noticed, the five attributes of MAX will help create many of the favorable cultural conditions listed, especially the "RAM It!" and "Prune It!" steps.

Weak cultures, on the other hand, are the result of complacent leaders who lead from their office chair and are prone to borrow credibility from accomplishments. They likewise ride economic momentum—going through the motions—rather than maintain the daily killer instinct necessary for building a high-performing culture. Traits common within such cultures may be any of the following (pretty much the opposite of the high-performing list):

- Unclear standards and expectations.
- Lots of gray area, confusion over what's expected, and poor communication overall.
- Entitled employees who believe tenure, experience, and credentials should substitute for today's results.
- Deadweight employees producing standards unworthy of the organization are tolerated.
- Inconsistent accountability.
- An *every man for himself* mentality.
- Peer pressure to conform and not to stand out.
- Sloppy and inconsistent processes.
- Also-ran customer experiences, resulting in below average customer retention, further resulting in high advertising expenditures to attract more customers for mediocre performers to abuse.
- A *just enough to get by and get paid* work ethic.
- Disengaged leaders who are aloof, inaccessible, unavailable, and indifferent.

At the end of the day, culture makes up a significant portion of a leader's report card, because it directly reflects the image of the person responsible for it. Strong products, robust consumer demand, and aggressive incentives can disguise cultural infections like those listed and the deficient leader creating or enabling them.

## The Second Quadrant of a Leader's Report Card: The People You've Attracted and Developed

As outlined in *Up Your Business*, the Business Law of Attraction states: *Leaders don't attract into their organization who they want, but who they are.* In other words, on a scale of 1 to 10, if a leader is a 6, he or she is not likely to have 9s and 10s lining up wanting to work for him or her. Rather, his or her team is probably filled with 3s, 4s, and 5s. Thus, the quality of people a leader attracts and develops speaks volumes about the leader himself or herself.

This is why it's puzzling when I hear leaders complaining about their lousy people. They are simply indicting themselves!

As with the cultural checklist, here's a quick list of benchmarks to measure this aspect of your leadership against:

- The team members grow under your leadership. They consistently improve skills, habits, and results.
- Negative, selfish, and divisive cultural cancers aren't tolerated, regardless of how high their production outcomes are.
- There is low team member turnover.
- People working for the leader often receive more responsibility or empowerment.
- The leader consistently trains, coaches, and mentors. He or she has installed these disciplines within the culture and views them as nonnegotiable, not something to get around to after all the so-called important stuff is done.

## The Third Quadrant of a Leader's Report Card: How You're Getting Results

Many executives or owners become so enamored when a leader gets results that they fail to look closely enough at *how* he or she is getting them. This creates blind spots as problems develop or persist with the manager, because the *how* shows where he or she is headed in the future. Because of the seducing effect results has on top executives, this quadrant may be the most overlooked of all. Here are some ways in which the *how* portends your, and the organization's, future:

- If you get results because you have built a great team made up of people who excel when you are away or off work, that's a reflection of several key leadership attributes. However, if you get results because you work 80 hours per week, never take a day off, and have made your people so dependent on you that they're useless when you're gone, you're headed for trouble (burnout and dis-engaged employees, for starters).
- If you get results because you have set clear expectations, have trained people to reach them, and hold them accountable for getting the job done, you're a rising star in the process of mastering the art of execution. If, on the other hand, you get results because you micromanage, threaten, bully, and berate people into

performing well, a train wreck of low morale, high turnover, and anemic credibility awaits you. It's only a matter of time.

- If you get results because you have a hot product and high demand, you may be vastly overestimating your own true abilities if you haven't built a foundation that makes success sustainable in the absence of such favorable conditions. If, however, you are getting results because you maximize each opportunity and have learned to play a poor hand well, you are demonstrating special abilities that mark you as one who is headed onward and upward.

In our fast-paced world we like to glance at results, see that they're good, declare that we have got it all figured out, and move on to what is next. But to accurately evaluate our or others' abilities, you have got to dig deeper into the *how*. It tells today's true story and predicts the future.

## The Fourth Quadrant of a Leader's Report Card: Performance versus Market

In a retail organization, for instance, if a product line's sales are up by 23 percent nationally, and your department is up by only 18 percent, you may have a problem (despite your natural tendency to want to celebrate an 18 percent increase). When a different line you represent is down 8 percent, but your department is flat, you may be demonstrating an exceptional ability that runs circles around your peers.

Performance versus market never tells the whole story behind a leader's results—or lack of results—but you must factor it into the four-quadrant big picture for the most insightful appraisal possible of a leader's true performance.

## Parting Thought

There are always exceptions: "We're unique because . . ." and other yeah-buts that can excuse, explain, or acclaim performance. This is why to get an accurate picture of your true abilities, you must evaluate all four of these factors: culture, people, the *how*, and market performance. Although there are a host of other helpful criteria, these four are simple, are easy to measure, and will go a long way in objectively assessing your performance and that of the other leaders in your organization, and in predicting the chances for execution excellence. *See? It's not rocket science!*

---

### Rocket Science Rant: The Truth about Drive and Stuff

A decades-old belief system—albeit a corrupt one—is that the deeper one goes into debt with lifestyle enhancements (toys and stuff), the more driven he or she becomes to make money. This mentality can start at the top of an organization and cascade throughout the ranks. I have personally known several leaders who admit delight in seeing their people overextend themselves financially so that they have to work extra shifts and days to maintain their lifestyle. Although it may be true that living with high overhead can stir up drive, it also creates stress—lots of it. Here are some examples of what happens to your stress level when you get caught up in the *work hard to get more stuff* trap:

1. First, you have to keep track of all your stuff.
2. Then you have to maintain and take care of your stuff.
3. You then have to insure your best stuff against loss.
4. You must also protect your stuff from people without as much stuff as you, who decide they want your stuff.
5. Naturally, the government will want tax overrides on your stuff, which makes you a slave not only to the stuff but to stuff-taxing bureaucrats, too.
6. Ironically, once you've had your stuff awhile, you're no longer happy with that old stuff and want bigger, better, more interesting stuff. And everywhere you look at your office and home, you find valuable space taken up by yesterday's stuff you no longer want, need, or appreciate.
7. It's also stressful when, despite your efforts to get great stuff, others don't notice, compliment, or fawn all over your stuff.
8. Inevitably, some friends or peers will get better stuff than you, which causes you to envy their stuff and no longer be content with your now inadequate stuff. The stuff you once sought and cherished now falls into the category of being not-up-to-snuff stuff.

9. After chasing stuff for decades, you finally realize that no matter how great your stuff is or how much stuff you have, there will always be someone who has more and better stuff than you. You hate this because you don't like to play games you can't win, and the stuff contest has no winner. It has only stressed-out and empty losers surrounded by not enough, or good enough, stuff.

10. As you grow older, you start to grasp that you can't take your stuff with you. So, deciding what will happen to your stuff when you're gone starts to stress you out even before you have to give your stuff up.

11. The people you do leave your stuff to will argue because they did not get the best stuff, or enough stuff. They will give some of your stuff to lawyers who promise to get them more of the stuff you left to someone else who also believes they got the short end of the stuff.

12. Some of the people you leave your stuff to will squander it, sell it, lose it through incompetence, or just plain screw up your stuff. The fact that your great stuff will fall into foolish hands causes you stress while the stuff is still yours and you're trying to enjoy it.

Despite my diatribe on stuff, don't get me wrong. I appreciate and enjoy nice cars, homes, vacations, and the like. I also don't believe there is anything wrong with having great stuff. But, over the years, as I've watched others become possessed by and obsessed with their possessions (losing peace, health, family, reputations, as well as their prized stuff) I've embraced a strategy of living beneath my means and generating drive through more productive, enjoyable, and fulfilling methods than the quest for the biggest and best stuff. Here are three of my favorites:

1. *Live to my maximum potential.* The never-ending journey to become more valuable, knowledgeable, disciplined, and skilled so that I am able to earn more. This drives me because, as I become more and earn more, I am better equipped to help causes and people important to me. This is far more exciting to me than lusting after the latest model Piaget or Bentley or a bigger beach house.

*(continued)*

(*continued*)
2. *Make a difference in the lives of others.* The opportunity and challenge to take what I'm becoming as outlined in the last point and pour it into others, leaving them better than when our paths first crossed, is a significant driver. It multiplies leadership, expands influence, and leaves a legacy.
3. *Give to those who cannot possibly give back.* This has become my parallel career, especially since starting the Matthew 25:35 Foundation with my wife, Rhonda, a few years ago and now having my daughter run it. We support food banks, orphans, antihuman-trafficking efforts, battered women's homes, homeless shelters, persecuted Christians, and prison ministries.

My daughter, Ashley, picked up on my sentiment toward too much stuff, and devised a fund-raising idea called Loot for Lives. It is a chance for people to donate stuff they don't want anymore, and our foundation will liquidate it, using the money to dig freshwater wells, build soup kitchens, and provide shelter for orphans around the world, especially in places such as Moldova, where street orphans are killed by organized crime rings, and their organs are harvested for profit. Yes, you read that right. It's one of the most repulsive acts imaginable, but it happens. And its practice is spreading into other parts of Europe.

Loot for Lives gave me an opportunity to put my money where my mouth was on my campaign against excess stuff, so, among other things, I donated three gold watches that spent more of their time languishing in a safe. It was easier than I thought to give up my two prized Piaget Polos and a rare Concord, $40,000 of stuff that no longer did it for me.

Now, lest you think I have taken a vow of poverty, intend to pass into monkhood, and retire to some cave, this is not the case. With God's grace, I plan to continue to grow our business and make even more money than before. Doing so will feed my three drivers as listed prior: becoming more personally valuable, adding value to others, and giving more to those who cannot give back. That's my plan and I'm sticking to it.

So, what drives you, Mr. or Ms. Leader? Actually, you don't have to answer a question like that aloud. Despite what you might say, where and how you spend your time, along with your checkbook and receipts, tell the real story of what drives you and what you value most.

# Part Two Summary

If you've flipped through the book, you might have noticed that this part on getting the leaders right is the lengthiest of the four. The reason? Until you and the other leaders on your team are embracing the philosophies and demonstrating the behaviors outlined in this chapter, no process will save you, not even master the art of execution (MAX). As I mentioned early on, "Get the Leaders Right!" should actually have been the first part of this book. But without presenting MAX first in its place, I couldn't have referred to the execution process throughout this part or show you how the two tie in.

So, now that you have a blueprint to improve your own leadership abilities, and those of the leaders you work with, you are better able to maximize the MAX process. Also, you are able to proceed into the next two parts concerning getting the culture right and getting the team right.

Part Two is all about looking in the mirror and recognizing what you are doing well so that you can stay on the right track, creating awareness of where you are off track, and equipping you with what's necessary to correct your course and lead at a higher level. We've covered a lot of ground in this part:

1. Do you overmanage and underlead?
2. Stretching, trenches, and changing.
3. You are the catalyst!
4. Buy-in is earned, not commanded.
5. Your baggage affects everyone's journey.
6. Get your *red belt* on!
7. The truth about mediocrity.

8. Beware the five seductions of leadership.

9. Five ways conventional wisdom destroys your potential.

10. The lost art of taking personal responsibility.

11. The power of preparation.

12. A blueprint for making the tough calls.

13. Four ways to measure your leadership.

14. The truth about drive and stuff.

I strongly advise that before you go on to Part Three, you review any key takeaways you had from these sections—your notes, underlines, or highlights. You're going to need every bit of insight and instruction from Part Two if you expect to progress through the next step successfully: getting the culture right.

Incidentally, if you've benefitted from the last two parts, why not pay it forward to someone else the book can help and post it on social media? Take a photo of the book, or a favorite thought or quote, and post it with your message. Copy me on Twitter @DaveAnderson100 and I'll hit you back and thank you personally.

# THREE
## PART

# GET THE CULTURE RIGHT!

$A$s a young sales manager, whenever I would attend training and hear a speaker begin talking about culture, I'd get turned off. I wasn't there to hear about a bunch of warm and fuzzy culture nonsense; I wanted to learn how to get the hard numbers. As the years passed and I wised up, I learned that you couldn't get hard, sustainable numbers without a supporting, "warm and fuzzy culture." The quality of one's cultural foundation makes the attainment of an organization's ultimate few objectives (TUFs) either feasible or impossible.

In this part I'm going to try to make the process of building a high-performance culture of execution (a culture where the right things are consistently done) very practical for you. I will outline five cultural pillars that comprise your organization's foundation and offer strategies for improving each one. Likewise, I will create a clear portrait of what the optimal culture looks like and offer specific concepts that must be woven into the foundation. In addition, I will present potential cultural infections and threats to your organization's foundation, as well as the strategies for preventing or removing them.

As the chapters progress you should clearly see how vital the right culture is in sustaining a process like master the art of execution (MAX) and how without it, MAX would never be fully leveraged, most likely fizzle into the fray, and become the latest failed flavor of the month.

Getting the culture right is a leader's responsibility, and as your own skills improve you will find that success in the cultural arena comes easier and faster. Getting the culture right also sets up the book's fourth strategy, "Get the Team Right!," because without question, a great culture is essential to attracting, developing, and retaining high-quality human capital.

Because culture requires constant attention and is never finished, it is best that we get to work! Although I believe you will find the strategies for getting the culture right simple—after all, it's not rocket science—that doesn't mean they will be easy. So, roll up your sleeves, and let's go tend to the essential, always-in-progress business of getting the culture right.

# CHAPTER 22

# Remember—It's the Culture, Stupid!

## The Challenge

Many organizations have an unhealthy addiction to silver bullets, quick fixes, and an array of flavors of the month that are offered as solutions to improve employee behaviors. These efforts range from monthly contests and sales gimmicks to threats and the latest peer-group best-idea bandwagon. Although versions of the aforementioned can cause a sudden spike in activity, they offer no long-term solutions for sustainable results. In fact, they often serve as a type of morphine used to numb the pain of mediocre results temporarily. But just as real morphine can be addictive (and too much of it can be lethal), these tricks have a similar effect on organizations. To grow an enterprise, there comes a time when it is necessary to stop killing the pain and have a surgery—not cosmetic surgery, but heart surgery. This means working strategically on the culture.

## Culture Is Execution's Foundation!

In the vernacular of organizations, "heart surgery" is about improving your culture so that it supports consistent execution and makes your team's ultimate few objectives (TUFs) attainable. In fact, whenever you're tempted to swallow some quick-fix Kool-Aid, not so gently remind yourself, "I don't need to chase another ploy, trend, or fad. I need to strengthen my organization's foundation. I don't want another 'seven-day diet.' I am committing to a lifestyle change; *it's the culture, stupid!*"

A surprising number of leaders foolishly consider culture as little more than an overrated buzzword promoted by academics or consultants and fail to recognize the vital role it plays in execution. To put culture's importance in perspective as execution's ally, consider the following:

- *Key Principle: Culture dictates behaviors, and behaviors determine results.* In other words, whatever execution efforts you're seeing consistently in your organization now are a result of the culture you have created. If you want to improve execution and results, you'll have to improve the culture first.

  In case you just skimmed point one, please reread it slowly because this principle is *big*. What it reveals is that the behaviors you're seeing consistently, in any given entity within your organization, are a result of the culture that you or some other leader has created. One of the biggest wastes of time you can engage in is trying to improve behaviors, execution, or results measurably without first changing the culture in which the behaviors are found.

  In my workshops and online courses on culture, I explain that to get your hands around improving your culture, first consider that it is made up primarily of five components: core values, mission, performance standards, core competencies, and people. These five cultural pillars make up the foundation of any organization. Just as you couldn't build a skyscraper on a foundation that is filled with cracks, is covered in holes, or is shifting on sand, neither can you expect sustainable increases in results without continuing to underpin your organization's cultural foundation.

- *Culture is never finished.* Building or strengthening a culture is not something you should ever cross off a to do list and declare as "mission accomplished." In fact, think of culture as you would a garden; a garden requires constant attention, and if you ignore it for long, the weeds, bugs, and disease will hijack the garden. The same is true for your culture. To remind my Twitter followers that culture requires constant attention, the first tip I send out Monday through Friday is a culture-building tip. You can review the tips @DaveAnderson100.

When you ignore the responsibility to continuously improve the five pillars of culture, you put your organization's health at risk. Here are signs that this is a current reality you need to face:

- Core values haven't been established, or, if they have, people aren't living them or being held accountable for them.
- No well-defined or compelling mission unites the team.
- There are no clearly written performance standards to achieve or consequences for failing to do so. This includes an absence of master the art of execution (MAX) acts for influencing high-impact behaviors daily.
- Core competencies are neither clearly identified nor leveraged.
- The wrong people have been hired and are being retained.

  Until these cultural failures are remedied, gimmicks, incentives, or threats of consequences that are used to improve execution will have a marginal shelf life.

- *Culture is both a leader's responsibility and report card.* A leader is the key shaper of the culture; culture truly is his or her report card. To take an accurate measure of your effectiveness, evaluate the improvement and vitality of the five cultural pillars in your primary areas of responsibility as we evaluate them in the upcoming chapters.
- *If you don't shape culture in your image, societal trends will shape it in their image.* Culture in an organization is innate. The question is: Who or what will shape it? If you don't shape your cultural foundation through your values, mission, standards, competencies, and quality people, then other things will. Those other things include societal trends, such as entitlement (everyone gets a trophy) and an absence of absolutes. Good luck executing when you find yourself burdened by those cultural infections.
- *A strong culture instills urgency, consistent execution, and accountability as fixed assets in your organization.* As you continue to refine

and strengthen your five cultural pillars, you won't need flavor-of-the-month stunts to create urgency, improve execution, or enhance accountability. These will naturally ensue as a result of the culture you have built.

Granted, diligently working on the five cultural pillars may not be as fancy or exciting as a new *hit it big quickly* scheme for your organization, but it is the key to execution excellence.

## Parting Thought

In the next few chapters I will dig more deeply into each of culture's five pillars and will present strategies for improving them. If you are tempted to take the shortcut by simply changing your TUFs, thinking this will change behaviors, think again. You can't change behaviors measurably or sustainably by simply raising or redefining objectives (by changing your vision, forecast, TUFs, objectives, or whatever else you want to call your goals). Imagine a new football coach taking over a winless team halfway through the season—a team burdened by a culture that lacks the right players, accountability, and strong values. It would be silly for this coach to say, "What this team needs is a new vision, and here it is: We're going to win the rest of our games this year." Consistent winning is not going to happen until the coach first fixes the culture. The same goes for you. With a strong culture in place, new TUFs will enhance, accelerate, and focus behaviors, but TUFs won't change them per se. The focus of this chapter is simple and clear: Whenever you are in doubt about where to begin to improve your business, remember . . . it's the culture, stupid! *See? It's not rocket science!*

(If you would like a free password to our three-hour How to Build a High Performance Culture virtual training course that normally retails for $39, e-mail itsnotrocketscience@learntolead.com with your request. Hurry though, this offer is subject to expire without further notice.)

# CHAPTER 23

# The Core Value Pillar

## The Challenge

Cultures are severely weakened when leaders tolerate toxic achievers (those who produce well but demonstrate deficient character). These team members are often talented and hardworking but are known for being selfish, divisive, dramatic, or disrespectful. Without clear and meaningful core values at the bedrock of culture, holding these folks accountable for executing within the parameters of expected behaviors rarely happens fast or often enough. To exacerbate matters, some organizations have core values, but no one even knows what they are! Other organizations have completely failed in this cultural responsibility and have never created core values at all. To master the art of execution, an organization must be staffed with people who demonstrate both competence and character. These people can produce desirable outcomes as well as exhibit desirable behaviors.

## Values Are Every Leader's Responsibility

Creating core values is not an intellectual exercise; rather, it is a vital leadership responsibility that reinforces the strength of your culture. However, until the values are lived, reinforced, and brought to life in your workplace, they are relegated to little more than management

**119**

talk without the walk. Following are baseline thoughts and strategies that explain why these values are important. I'm also including five core values with examples of how my company, LearnToLead, uses them as a filter for hiring, firing, and decision making.

1. *Core values are nonnegotiable behaviors that broadcast what you expect from your employees as well as what you are unwilling to compromise on.* These behavioral expectations are just as essential as performance expectations.

2. *Core values establish an accountability benchmark that is essential to building and maintaining a high-performance culture.* Along with vision, mission, and performance standards, core values are an essential component of corporate clarity.

3. *Core values are validated and brought to life when the leaders live them personally, thereby making certain their behaviors embody the values rather than mock them.*

4. *The importance of core values is also highlighted when leaders tie both positive and unproductive behaviors into the values:*

> *The leader, speaking publicly at a team meeting:* "John really lived our teamwork value yesterday. Sue had fallen behind on her reports, and John stayed after work to help her catch up and had a great attitude about it. No one even had to ask him to do it, and he didn't ask for anything in return. If everyone in this room consistently demonstrates this kind of behavior, we'll blow our TUFs [ultimate few objectives] out of the water this quarter."
>
> *The leader, speaking in private to a values violator:* "Alex, the way you just spoke to that customer violates our integrity value. Frankly, if everyone spoke to customers in that manner, we wouldn't stay in business very long. Let me show you again the proper way to handle that situation. In addition I will expect you to do it that way from now on."

5. *Core values should be both memorable and few.* Quality is more important than quantity. Remember, many of your values will cover a lot of other ground. For instance, if a core value is integrity, you don't also need values for meeting deadlines,

keeping commitments, or being to work on time. Integrity covers all of this and much more.

6. *If your core values don't influence the daily behaviors of your people, they are impotent.* When values are brought to life by a leadership team that champions them and personally lives them out, employees will have more confidence making decisions and handling certain situations without checking with supervisors. This accelerates their own growth, morale, and results.

7. *A core value should be further explained by demonstrating what the value looks like when it is being lived.* A brief and descriptive sentence is effective in this regard. So you may see what I mean, I'm including LearnToLead's five core values and their subsequent descriptive sentences.

   *Teamwork:* The good of the team comes before the personal pride, comfort level, or agenda of any one individual.

   *Integrity:* We will always do what is right; not what is easy, cheap, popular, or convenient. And we will do so without excuse and regardless of the cost.

   *Urgency:* We will honor and serve one another and customers with urgency, because there is power in now. Later is too late!

   *Personal growth:* We will work as hard on ourselves as we do on our job, because our business will get better when we get better. Not getting better is not an option!

   *Attention to detail:* We will become brilliant in the basics and commit to doing the ordinary things extraordinarily well. We are committed to becoming faithful in the "little" things, because in pursuit of perfection, we can expect to catch excellence.

## Your Corporate DNA

Core values comprise your corporate DNA; they reveal volumes about who you are, what you stand for, and what you are unwilling to settle for. Reassess your values and, if necessary, reintroduce them to the team. Admit that you haven't done a good enough job in the past of communicating the key behaviors your organization expects and celebrates and commit to do better moving forward. Consider discussing a value of the week during team meetings. Go over the definition, discuss what the value looks like in practice, point out individuals who have lived it recently, and discuss how the team can do more to bring it to life in the future.

I also recommend that you place your values and definitions in writing and review them at the appropriate time when interviewing people. Let them know up front what you are about and how you will expect them to conduct themselves. It's foolish to hire someone, spring the values on him or her later, and basically say, "Surprise! I hope you can live up to these because they are important here!"

Once your values are established credibly as one of your five pillars of culture, you will also have an easier time spotting who needs to change his or her behaviors and who may no longer fit on the team at all. In fact, one reason why leaders tend to keep the wrong people too long is because not enough clear and credible criteria make it obvious sooner that the person is a poor fit—a cultural infection of sorts that needs to go away. In the case of our company, we don't have trouble with employees coming in late to work for long. Why? They'd be violating four of our five values: teamwork, integrity, urgency, and attention to detail. Likewise, because our values are credible, there is no way I could justify keeping an employee with tardiness issues and at the same time expect the values or my own leadership to have any credibility. Thus, core values strengthen and protect our cultural foundation, influencing productive behaviors daily and steadily moving us toward TUFs' attainment.

## Parting Thought

Just as all organizations have cultures (the only question being "What is it?") all organizations have core values. They're official and powerful, existent but impotent, or undefined and unspoken but well understood (more bluntly put, "Cover your own behind and watch your own back because nobody else will"). To master the art of execution, not only must you inculcate core values into your culture, but also your people must live them out in their interactions with both colleagues and customers. If you are the leader and your values aren't what they should be, it is your own fault. The good news is that you can fix it. The guidelines given here are simple, and they offer a great place for you to start. *See? It's not rocket science!*

# CHAPTER 24

# The Mission Pillar

## The Challenge

In many organizations, team members and sometimes entire departments unwittingly work against one another because they're not united behind a common purpose—a mission. They have different ideas of what the team's mission is, or, in the absence of it being clearly established and communicated, they conjure up their own. These out-of-sync behaviors create numerous potholes on the road to executing an organization's ultimate few objectives (TUFs). Just as with core values, in the absence of a clear and unifying mission, team members aren't sure enough about what to say yes or no to daily, what to engage in or withdraw from, what is a priority, and what shouldn't be done at all. The resulting chaos in the cubicles divides a team's power, breaks its momentum, squanders its resources, lowers its morale, and sabotages its results.

## Mission's Role in Vision

Mission and vision are frequently confused more often than they should be. Vision is a specific direction. It comprises your TUFs and is most likely synonymous with your TUFs. It is a specific and

123

quantifiable outcome that you desire to attain. Mission is your organization's purpose. Living your mission should take you to your vision. *Mission* is defined as "any important task or duty that is assigned, allotted, or self-imposed. An important goal or purpose that is accompanied by strong conviction" (*Dictionary.com*, n.d.). For example, at LearnToLead we have new TUFs each year, but our mission remains constant: "to provide the tools and inspiration our clients need to reach their personal and corporate potential . . . and to always look for an opportunity to do something extra for them throughout the process." We believe that through daily execution of master the art of execution (MAX) and living our mission, we will reach our TUFs. In other words—just as with all pillars of culture—the mission pillar must align with and support the TUFs, or you will fall short.

### Three Problems with Mission Statements

1. *Most mission statements are mission chapters or paragraphs that fail to communicate concisely to the team what its purpose is.* Frankly, if your people cannot articulate your mission, they are not likely to be able to execute it.

2. *Another problem with mission statements is that many organizations act as though once they have created one, their job in that regard is finished.* But, just like with core values, mission must be brought to life within a culture so that it can influence behaviors, serve as a decision-making filter, and clarify focus and purpose. Team members should also be able to see how their MAX acts align with the behaviors necessary to live out the mission and reach the TUFs.

3. *A third issue with mission statements is that the majority of team members couldn't recite theirs accurately if their jobs depended on it.* As with core values, when suffering at the hands of inattentive leadership, mission statements are relegated to fancy wall décor—academic busywork dreamt up by well-intentioned leaders who failed to bring their mission's heartbeat to life meaningfully throughout the organization. Thus, the cultural foundation develops cracks that are caused by competing agendas, confusion as to an individual's roles and goals, and diminished accountability for expected behaviors.

## Parting Thought

If your mission statement is too long or complicated to be effective, then you must simplify it. If it exists but only a few know it or live it, then relaunch it. If you don't have one, then for goodness' sake, do your job and create it so that your cultural foundation is firmed up, behaviors become more focused, the team becomes more united, and the TUFs become more attainable. To get things moving, ask yourself, "Why do we exist as an organization?" The answer will embody your purpose. *See? It's not rocket science!*

# CHAPTER 25

# The Performance Standard Pillar

## The Challenge

Lack of accountability weakens a culture and renders execution of daily master the art of execution (MAX) acts inconsistent or even optional in some team members' eyes. A key reason why accountability is missing in so many organizations is because of unclear performance standards. Because ambiguity is the enemy of accountability, lack of clear performance standards creates a serious cultural flaw. Although some organizations do an okay job of defining the ultimate few objectives (TUFs), desired outcomes, they falter in establishing the daily performance standards, MAX acts, that make TUFs' attainment possible. To make matters worse, standards are often too low, not in writing, and without appropriate consequences for execution failure. Thus, many leaders dupe themselves into believing they have performance *standards* when all they have in reality are performance *suggestions.*

## Performance Standards versus Performance Suggestions

Lest you think I'm splitting hairs by differentiating between standards and suggestions, please consider *Dictionary.com*'s description of each:

- *Standard:* "a rule or principle that is used as a basis for judgment" (n.d). This powerful definition implies that a standard is specific and official enough for you to hold someone accountable for it and apply consequences for failure if necessary.
- *Suggestion:* "something suggested, as a piece of advice" (n.d.). Advice implies that what you *expect* to be done does not necessarily *have* to. It suggests that your expectations are optional and don't have to be taken seriously. Needless to say, performance suggestions portend disastrous consequences for your culture, execution, and results.

## Performance Standard Checklist

Although pillars such as mission and core values can remain constant in organizations with only occasional tweaking, performance standards should change as often as necessary to maintain their relevance. MAX acts that in one season were vital to performance may be rendered impotent as markets or competitors change, as supply and demand for your products or services fluctuates, or as economic conditions vary. Following are seven simple rules that summarize what you can do to improve the performance standard pillar of your culture.

1. *Performance standards should be in writing and acknowledged with a sign-off from an employee.* This helps team members become more successful by creating clearer targets for them to hit. It gets both you and them on the same page, eliminates gray areas, and takes away any excuses of ignorance from each employee concerning what was expected from him or her. It eliminates the pervasive loser's limps, such as, "I didn't know that's what you expected; you have to be clearer; I'm not a mind reader" and subsequent nonsense underperformers belch out in an attempt to shift blame onto you for their failures.

2. *Performance standards should have specific metrics that can be measured accurately.* "Work hard every day" is not a standard; it is a suggestion (advice). "Average 12 sales per month" is a standard. Although the importance of specificity was stressed in point one, especially in relation to TUFs and MAX acts, it bears repeating here because people, especially poor performers, will manipulate gray areas concerning performance. This is why in strong cultures, the standards are so clear that there is nowhere for the laggards to hide. Your rhythm of accountability meetings (RAMs) will go a long way in creating this reality and reinforcing accountability to strengthen the performance standard pillar.

3. *Performance standards should include a blend of activity and outcome expectations.* Activity expectations may be MAX acts, such as $x$ number of shown appointments per day. Outcome expectations could include one of the organization's TUFs, such as actual sales volume.

4. *You should present performance standards in a manner that creates an expectation that they are subject to revision, additions, and deletions over time.* By presenting standards in this manner (similar to how PSPs were presented), you do not lose credibility when you decide to change them for any reason in the future.

5. *You should strengthen your nonnegotiable performance standards, be they MAX acts or individual TUFs, with preestablished consequences for failure.* The consequences are up to you, but you should not overlook them, because they are essential to protecting your culture. For instance, if you have a MAX act that someone must make $x$ number of calls to customers per day, you might consider a progressive form of discipline to address a failure to execute as follows:

   a. First offense results in a verbal reminder.

   b. Second offense results in a written warning.

   c. Third offense results in an unpaid, one-week suspension.

   d. Fourth offense results in termination.

   Again, this is merely an example. Customize the consequences to fit your needs.

6. *You should bring performance standards to life by discussing them often: in training meetings, in one-on-one coaching sessions, and*

*during performance reviews.* This keeps them at the forefront of the team's mind and strengthens their credibility.

7. *Performance standards are effective when presented as a baseline level of performance required, not as heroic.* To build a second-mile culture, people must understand that the standards you're establishing are the minimum required. They must understand that ultimately, you'll evaluate team members by their ability to exceed expectations consistently.

These seven guidelines aren't the final word on performance standard pointers, but they are a great start. Use them to evaluate your own. If necessary, redefine your performance standards, and reintroduce them to the team as soon as possible.

## Parting Thought

You should always introduce new standards in a collaborative manner that says, "I'm on your side, and I want to help you become more successful." They should never come across as a threat. By keeping them simple, you will help each team member improve his or her daily focus by establishing clearer targets for him or her to shoot for. In addition, you will eliminate gray areas, put yourself and the team on the same page (one that is synergistic), and improve your own leadership credibility. This one cultural pillar provides a plethora of essential benefits! All you must do is decide, define, and then communicate what you want most from each person on your team in the first place. *See? It's not rocket science!*

# CHAPTER 26

# Establish Your
# *Business Facts of Life*

## The Challenge

Organizations with unclear core values and performance expectations abound. Lack of clarity invites a sense of entitlement that infects the culture and makes consistent execution a pipe dream. Even when expectations are given, they often don't directly affect the most desired or necessary behaviors within a culture. Thus, they may influence behaviors but not necessarily the ones that matter most.

## If You Don't Make Waves, You'll Drown

In my book *If You Don't Make Waves, You'll Drown: 10 Hard-Charging Strategies for Leading in Politically Correct Times* (John Wiley & Sons 2005), I outlined 25 sample facts of life. Business facts of life (BFOL) are no-nonsense, no-gray-area, and non-negotiable expectations that focus team members on the behaviors that are most essential to reaching the ultimate few objectives (TUFs). In the subsequent paragraphs, I offer sample BFOL

**131**

customized specifically in support of master the art of execution (MAX) to ensure that the most vital daily behaviors are made clear enough to all team members up front. As you consider the following 12, feel free to use or tweak any or all to strengthen the core value or performance standard pillars:

### Sample MAX BFOL

1. You are expected to know, and be able to recite, those TUFs most relevant to your particular department or division.

   *If we're not on the same page, we are unconsciously working against one another.*

2. You are expected to understand and execute your daily, weekly, and monthly MAX acts as a priority, with excellence, and without excuse.

   *You needn't do anything extraordinary each day, but, you will do the ordinary extraordinarily well and do so consistently.*

3. You are expected to treat each day as the potential masterpiece that it is. Your objective is never to *get through* the day but to *get from* the day!

   *When you are doing poorly, you will correct the course quickly. When you're winning, you'll run up the score.*

4. You are expected to own the results of your MAX board and focus on what you can control during a rhythm of accountability meeting (RAM). When missing your objectives, you will make commitments you fully intend to keep and not just say what you believe others want to hear.

   *You will depend on better daily decisions to get your results and not rely on conditions that are beyond your control.*

5. I expect you to act on the feedback you are given concerning your performance. When the company invests time and effort into your development, it's essential to see a return.

   *Feedback is an opportunity to adjust and grow. Don't waste it!*

6. You are expected to apply pruning principles consistently for the sake of improving execution efficiency. Pruning is evidence of your desire to improve continuously.

   *Never miss an opportunity to realign, revitalize, or remove what is not optimal to the organization's success.*

7. Our organization's mission defines our purpose. You are expected to know it, and live it, by fulfilling your role in it every day.
   *By living our mission we will achieve, our TUFs.*

8. Our core values are mandates, not suggestions. You are expected to make decisions and demonstrate behaviors that align with them daily.
   *Do not expect us to compromise our values to suit your perform-ance or preferences.*

9. You may fully expect to receive everything you earn and deserve. *Earn* means to acquire through merit; *deserve* means to be worthy of or to qualify for.
   *Expecting that which you haven't earned or deserved demonstrates a sense of entitlement we will not tolerate in our culture.*

10. Although your best efforts are appreciated, you will ultimately be measured by your results.
    *Tenure, credentials, experience, or best efforts do not substitute for results.*

11. You are expected to become brilliant in the basics of your job and to execute them every day—and every day means every day (EDMED)!
    *Forego the quest for silver bullets, and successfully execute one 3.5-yard run after the other, day in and day out.*

12. You are expected to be on time to all meetings, especially to RAMs.
    *Being late is both an arrogant choice and a breach of your personal integrity.*

There are certainly other BFOL, which you can add to strengthen the performance standard pillar and support your efforts to master the art of execution. The preceding 12 are just a sampling, not the final word.

## Parting Thought

Put your own version of the BFOL in writing to create clarity, focus, unity, and a benchmark for greater accountability, all while reinforc-ing both MAX and the culture that supports it. Go over them with each team member, and have him or her sign off to affirm that you are both are on the same page. Make sure they all have the training and tools to execute them, and hold them accountable for doing so. Expect to see far greater results in your organization. *See? It's not rocket science!*

---

### Rocket Science Rant: "Fat, Drunk, and Stupid" Are Not Ways to Run an Organization

A classic scene from the 1978 movie *Animal House* was created when Faber College dean Vernon Wormer disgustedly addressed the failing grades of the delinquent Delta Tau Chi fraternity members as follows:

**Dean Vernon Wormer:** "Here are your grade point averages. Mr. Kroger: two Cs, two Ds, and an F. That's a 1.2. Congratulations, Kroger. You're at the top of the Delta pledge class. Mr. Dorfman?"

**Flounder [Dorfman]:** [*drunk*] "Hello!"

**Dean Vernon Wormer:** "0.2 . . . Fat, drunk, and stupid is no way to go through life, son." (IMDb, n.d.)

Fat, drunk, and stupid Flounder was actually fortunate to have a leader who cared enough to confront his failure bluntly. Because *Animal House* was set in 1962, Dean Wormer was far less constrained by today's politically correct censorship. Today a court-appointed counselor would likely reassure pathetic Flounder that his sorry state wasn't his fault; his mother, his father, or his teachers would be the scapegoats for his 0.2 GPA, and Dean Wormer would most likely be sent to jail.

John Vernon, who played Dean Wormer, passed in 2005. If he were addressing an underperforming organization today, he'd find it necessary to assail some members in a manner similar to the way he assailed Flounder, perhaps with something like: "Mr. or Mrs. Leader: Fat, drunk, and stupid is no way to run your organization."

What exactly does it mean to try to build a high-performing culture and master the art of execution while being fat, drunk, and stupid? Here are parallels. Those that make you most uncomfortable have something to teach you.

- **Fat.** You've gotten complacent because your results are so good. Your personalized success profiles (PSPs) are out of date and irrelevant, RAMs are inconsistent, and you don't prune deadweight; rather, you've learned to live with it because overall, you're making money, so why rock the boat? Besides, who has the time to recruit someone new and then train him or her when business is rockin'?
- **Drunk. As I mentioned when presenting the red belt mindset,** success is an intoxicant, and intoxicated people don't face reality very well. Here are five quick examples:
  - You justify keeping toxic achievers who hit the numbers even though they abuse your values.
  - You spend more time with stuff than with people; after all, you have earned the right to that nice office and intend to roost there as often as possible.
  - Because you're doing so well, training is no longer as necessary as it once was. After all, you have a team filled with veterans who know what they're supposed to do.
  - You no longer read leadership books or attend courses, because your track record of success speaks for itself. You're convinced it's all right to take what you learned once upon a time and stretch it out for the rest of your career.
  - Your team is far better than most, so you're chasing six TUFs this year, rather than the recommended maximum of three. If anyone can do it, if there is an exception to the rule, it's certainly you and your elite bunch.
- **Stupid.** Stupidity in an organization is demonstrated when you read a chapter like this, which makes you aware of the fact that you have become fat and drunk, but decide to do nothing about it. You are intrigued and entertained by these concepts but think they apply to the other guy and blissfully go about business as usual, thinking, "Perhaps I am above that which others must abide by." Although you would never say something so arrogant aloud, your inaction says it for you.

*(continued)*

(*continued*)

You may even boast that you don't employ half of the disciplines mentioned in this book but are still successful. For the third time in this book thus far I'll remind you that you are successful *despite* your behaviors—acting fat and drunk, not *because* you have gotten fat and drunk. If you dwell in this state of delusion, you should be warned and reminded that the universal laws of sowing and reaping really do apply to you. Likewise, just because you don't see immediate consequences for your failed disciplines does not mean that you will escape them. You may be in the grace period between becoming fat or drunk and actually suffering stupidity-induced decline. The good news is if you find yourself here, you can still turn things around if you recommit to healthy disciplines and abandon the self-destructive practices that threaten your future.

Incidentally, most leaders in an organization get fat and drunk from time to time. The objective should be to learn from it, to get back on track, and not to permit stupidity to become a lifestyle. Although being fat and drunk is certainly reckless, costly, and irresponsible, staying stupid will eventually terminate either your organization as a whole or your role there as a leader.

# CHAPTER 27

# The Core Competency Pillar

## The Challenge

Leaders commonly take their organizations' strengths for granted; they do so precisely because they are strong. As a result, they divert resources and talent away from these core competencies and into marginal areas—their weaknesses. Although you shouldn't ignore your weaknesses, ignoring your strengths makes reaching your fullest potential impossible. In fact, although working on your weaknesses may help you get by, it's leveraging your strengths (your core competencies) that can lift you to greatness. Here is a major problem with investing too much time in weaknesses: You feel like you are always playing catch-up, are coming from behind, and never have the upper hand on execution momentum as you pursue the ultimate few objectives (TUFs). Oftentimes you're not even playing to win; rather, you're just trying not to give up the ground you have gained in the past. The results of this choice include frustration, stress, and lack of fulfillment.

## The Big Three

Thus far, I have presented three of the five pillars of culture:

1. Core values
2. Mission
3. Performance standards

Core competencies are aspects of your enterprise and components of your culture that a peer or competitor would look at and say, "I wish we did *x* as well as they do." Core competencies may cover an array of areas, such as hiring, training, follow-up, customer retention, inventory turn, or employee engagement. In addition to building on the competencies you currently have, to differentiate your culture from competitors completely, it's essential that you weave the following three core competencies into your culture if you have not already done so.

### Core Competency 1: Attracting and Developing Great People within Your Organization

Part Four of this book, "Get the Team Right!," will give numerous insights into building this core competency. Without question, until you get the right people on your team and work to develop them to their fullest potential, all other aspects important to your organization will fall short: creating great customer experiences, executing master the art of execution (MAX) acts with excellence and consistency, training (training undriven or talentless people brings little return), et cetera.

### Core Competency 2: Delivering Extreme Differentiation in the Customer Experience

Naturally, without the right people this is not going to happen. But with motivated, competent, and talented people, training that addresses how to deliver great customer experiences, and a MAX process to ensure execution in that regard is consistent, you can pull away from the pack in your industry. In fact there's little doubt that nothing is more memorable in a positive way to a customer, or makes price less relevant to that customer, than the *wow* experiences they have in dealing with an organization's people. On the other hand, without the right people, training, or execution process, the customer will still have a memorable experience. It just won't be one you want him or her telling others about in an online review.

## Core Competency 3: Mastering the Art of Execution

Surely, the third core competency doesn't surprise you at this point. Training great people to deliver great customer experiences and having them work daily within the MAX process is the perfect storm of core competencies that can put your organization into a league of your own. When I use the term *league of your own*, I'm not referring to being number one in your league. A league of your own means you get so good at what you do that you create a different league, and you're the only one in it; there's you, and then there's everybody else. You are peerless—the ultimate goal for any organization. (To view a free video clip of me explaining the *league of your own* concept to a live audience, visit the Insider Club at LearntoLead.com.)

Attracting and developing great people within your organization, delivering extreme differentiation in the customer experience, and mastering the art of execution are dependent upon each other. For example, you cannot expect to deliver *wow* customer experiences with indifferent or incompetent team members. You can have great people who have never been trained to deliver extreme differentiation in the customer experience, but they will consistently fall short of getting the wow. You may have outstanding human capital and intensive training on how to get the wow, but without a process like MAX to execute your plan consistently, you'll find yourself frequently frustrated as you fall short of greatness, despite your most laborious efforts.

## Parting Thought

No organization just gets lucky and becomes great. Rather, entities reaching league-of-their-own status are built by design, with the right decisions and disciplines being repeated daily over time. Failure isn't a matter of good luck or bad luck either. Mediocre organizations are built over time as well, with wrong decisions and letups in disciplines being repeated daily over time. It's your choice whether to focus on and build the three core competencies into your culture outlined here that will help your organization become a league of its own. As we discussed in Part Two, "Get the Leader Right!," a fish rots at the head; it all comes back to you. Yes, you. In the words of Martha Reeves and the Vandellas, "Nowhere to run to, baby, nowhere to hide." *See? It's not rocket science!*

# CHAPTER 28

# The People Pillar

## The Challenge

Many leaders focus more on their goals and strategies than they do on the quality of the people they're counting on to execute and get them there. Here's the problem with that: A great dream with the wrong team is a nightmare. A great dream with mediocre people will bring you mediocre results. If you're at a point where your dreams—the ultimate few objectives (TUFs)—are bigger than your team, then you have got to either grow up the team or give up the dreams. Without question, people are the most important pillar of your culture. They must share your core values, believe in your mission, have the competence to meet your performance standards, and have the talent to align with your core competencies. Because the book's final chapters in "Get the Team Right!" will offer in-depth strategies for developing people, here we'll review numerous ways people affect every aspect of your organization's culture and how culture in turn affects the people working within it. The relevance of the connection is unmistakable and should strongly influence how and where you spend more time—building culture and people.

## How Culture Affects People and People Affect Culture

- People in a strong culture share common beliefs, customs, and language, forging an even closer bond among team members.
- People who are highly developed more naturally attract other highly developed people into their culture.
- People are far more likely to be strongly engaged in a high-performance culture.
- People define your culture. In a customer's eyes people are the most memorable (for better or worse) aspect of their customer experience.
- People want to work in a culture where they have a chance to become more as a human being.
- People want to work in a culture where they are part of something special.
- People want to work in a culture where they have a chance to make a difference in the lives of others, in their industry, and in their community.
- People who don't share your values are cancers that will destroy your culture.
- People who are made clear as to what your values are, and who are convinced you're serious about them, make faster and more confident decisions.
- People unsure of your mission will unconsciously work against one another as they pursue their own agendas.
- People unsure of your mission will become territorial and will create unhealthy competition for resources, power struggles, and turf wars.
- People unclear about your performance standards will become entitled, unaccountable, irresponsible, indifferent, and stagnant.
- To reach organizational TUFs, your job is to get people better or get better people. In most cases you can expect to do both.
- People who are unclear about TUFs and master the art of execution (MAX) acts will mistake motion for progress and live most days active but unaccomplished.

- People will more consistently deliver second-mile performances when they work in a culture with performance standards that are clear, compelling, and high.
- People are distracted and demoralized by cultural misfits (those who are incompetent or lack the right character).
- The wider the gap between your top and bottom performers, the weaker your culture will become.
- People with the right character are far more likely to remain employed working in an organization that has created a high-performing culture.
- People expect their leader to step up and do whatever is necessary to protect the special culture they've helped build.

## Parting Thought

Culture attracts what it is, not what it wants. By diligently improving the other four pillars of culture, you will naturally and dramatically improve the people already there. In turn, by hiring the right people, you will naturally and dramatically improve the culture. Which is most important or which must come first? You need to do both, so take your pick and get after it. *See? It's not rocket science!*

# CHAPTER 29

# The Earn and Deserve Culture

## The Challenge

"Pay attention to your culture," "You need to strengthen your culture," and "Your culture needs some work" are statements most would find reasonable and difficult to argue with. However, their general nature leaves much to be desired. After all, most leaders know what they should do; they simply don't know how to do it, don't do it, or don't do it consistently. This is why in the following pages I am going to present specific words, concepts, and mind-sets that you must weave into a high-performance culture. I will also offer specific words, concepts, and mind-sets that you must weed out of culture to strengthen its foundation. My goal is to help you by creating a portrait of the ideal culture by supplying specific examples of what must exist within a high-performing culture as well as what must be eliminated. Although you may never reach the ideal culture, the very act of striving toward it will lift you to far higher levels than you would have reached otherwise.

## Earn and Deserve at the Bedrock

According to class attendees, one of the most helpful parts of my Up Your Business 2.0 Super Leadership workshop is when I have attendees create two columns on a page, writing "Strong Cultural Words to Weave In" on one side of the page and "Weak Cultural Words to Weed Out" on the other side. Over the course of the two days, I add to the list, making a blueprint of the mind-sets, values, attitudes, and behaviors you must embed in a great culture, as well as the destructive mind-sets, values, attitudes, and behaviors you must remove. The two words I begin this journey with on the "strong" column are always the same—*earn* and *deserve*. These words form the bedrock of a high-performing culture. Their definitions, which tell the real story, are as follows:

> *Earn:* "To acquire through merit" (*Dictionary.com*, n.d.).
> *Deserve:* "To be worthy of, qualified for, or have a claim to reward" (*Dictionary.com*, n.d.).

An *earn and deserve culture* is integral to mastering the art of execution because it promotes merit and accountability while it repels entitlement and sloth. It sends the message that all team members will receive rewards, opportunities, promotions, and discretion in accordance with what they have acquired through merit, what they are worthy of, and what they have qualified for. Consider the following dialogue and contemplate the message it sends concerning what your culture is about:

> "Boss, why didn't I get an end-of-the-year-raise?"

> "Because you didn't earn it. You failed to acquire it through merit. In our culture we reward results, not requests—stepping up versus showing up. Let's sit down and redefine expectations so you'll more clearly understand how to qualify for, and be worthy of, additional compensation."

Or . . .

> "Boss, I'd like the next shot at management; after all I've been here the longest."

"I sincerely appreciate your interest in advancing in our organization; however, in our culture we reward results over tenure. The person we promote will be the man or woman who is most qualified for, and worthy of, additional responsibilities. I'm happy to lay out for you exactly what you can do to earn and deserve a shot at future promotions."

As I do during my workshops, I'm going to balance words that work in culture with those that hurt culture to help create a well-rounded portrait of what you're both moving toward and moving away from. Thus, the first three words, mind-sets, and concepts you must work to weed out of your culture are the three amigos of misery: *fault*, *blame*, and *excuse*. Here are their definitions.

*Fault*: "Responsibility for failure" (*Dictionary.com*, n.d.).

*Blame*: "To place the responsibility for (a fault, error, etc.)" (*Dictionary .com*, n.d.).

*Excuse*: "A plea offered in extenuation of a fault or for release from an obligation, promise, etc." (*Dictionary.com*, n.d.).

Here's an example of how an employee might use the words in a sentence (something you might have heard a time or two): "It's not my fault I had a bad month. I blame the weather, the economy, the time of year, the inventory, the advertising, the incompetents I work with, and the competition. Plus, you don't really motivate me." They'd then undoubtedly follow with an excuse to explain why this is the case.

Undoubtedly, if someone of this nature were to accept responsibility for his or her poor month, he or she would probably have to confess some of the following: "I had a bad month because I am lazy, don't control my attitude, lack discipline, and fail to plan, prepare, prospect, practice, follow up, ask for referrals, or learn more about my profession."

Sadly, purveyors of blame fail to realize that blame is the anti-focus, stripping them of personal power as they focus their attention on things they cannot affect and ignore those they can. When they make excuses, they demonstrate the DNA of underachievers.

Fault, blame, and excuses are a trio of cultural travesties that tie together to create a pathetic progression of palaver designed to remove the burden of success from one's shoulders. "It's not *my fault*, so I must *blame* someone or something else and then create an *excuse* to explain why." Fault, blame, and excuses create cultural decay. If they pervade your culture, it's the leadership's fault. Leaders are to blame and have no excuse for permitting their existence. Although it's probably obvious to you at this point, the best antidote for the *fault, blame, excuse* mind-set is to create an *earn and deserve* culture where people are held accountable (where they can expect to get everything they acquire through merit, through being worthy of, and through qualifying for).

## Parting Thought

If you want to change your culture, you need to change the conversations within it. Discuss with your other leaders where you see people wanting what they haven't earned or deserved. Ask yourself, "What have I been giving too easily to my employees that has entitled them?" Now, realize you must set up new parameters that cause them to earn and deserve these things. Discuss also who has been blaming and making excuses to shift the spotlight off their incompetence and onto people or things they can't control. These first five words (earn, deserve, fault, blame, and excuse) have a total of seven simple syllables; they're simple, we get them, and we understand their power to either elevate or devastate cultures. By focusing on weaving the first two into your culture while you weed out the latter three, you take a significant step forward in getting the process, leaders, culture, and people right. *See? It's not rocket science!*

# CHAPTER 30

# The Ideal Cultural Portrait

## *Consistent in, Mediocre Out*

### The Challenge

Inconsistency, the failure to take responsibility, and the tolerance of mediocrity devastates culture. Despite this, leaders often major in all three offenses: They do the right things when it's easy, cheap, popular or convenient; they fall into the blame game as described in our last chapter; and they are prone to rationalize, trivialize, sanitize, and compromise with what is mediocre, rather than deal with it. As our cultural portrait continues, this chapter will discuss the importance of weaving in consistency as it relates to your cultural foundation, while revitalizing or removing—pruning—what is mediocre. Both disciplines are essential parts of getting the culture right and the primary responsibilities of leadership.

## Why Organizations Fail to Reach Their Potential

While appearing on MSNBC's show *Your Business*, I was asked if I believed that the number one reason why organizations didn't reach their fullest potential was because they failed to change. I replied that although failing to change was a common reason, my experience had shown that the top reason organizations fall short of their potential is chronic inconsistency. They would in fact change but then not stick with it. Then, they would try another initiative, change again, but fail to follow through. This brings us to our third cultural concept that must be weaved into culture:

> *Consistent:* "Constantly adhering to the same principles, course, form, etc." (*Dictionary.com*, n.d.).

Consistent organizations are filled with people who are brilliant in the basics of their job both day in and day out. They go the extra mile on days they feel like it and even when they don't, even when it's not easy, cheap, popular, or convenient. In fact, if you study good performers and organizations, and compare them to great ones, you'll find that both groups do many of the same things. The great ones just do them more consistently. Because of this, they do things with greater excellence, strengthen their culture, and pull away from the pack.

Frankly, even a sluggard can manage to do the right things occasionally on good days when he or she feels like it. But leaders in a high-performance culture identify daily, weekly, and monthly disciplines that must be executed consistently without excuse, and they hold people accountable for doing so. These leaders understand that no organization can become great by doing what matters most every once in a while.

Although *consistent* is a word to weave into your high-performing culture, you are also charged with revitalizing or removing what is mediocre. *Mediocre* is defined as "of only ordinary or moderate quality; neither good nor bad; barely adequate" (*Dictionary.com*, n.d.).

Many leaders believe themselves to have high standards and to have already built high-performance cultures. Maybe, maybe not. Considering how repulsive the label attached to the word *mediocre* probably is to you, honestly evaluate your culture and determine the following:

- How many average, ordinary, or not outstanding performers remain on your payroll, and why?
- How many average, ordinary, or not outstanding strategies, policies, and procedures do you continue to stick with, and why?
- Which average, ordinary, or not outstanding daily activities do you engage in that distract you from executing your master the art of execution (MAX) acts, cause you to postpone your rhythm of accountability meetings (RAMs), or make you procrastinate concerning pruning disciplines that are long overdue for attention?
- Which average, ordinary, or not outstanding belief systems do you hang on to that permit these situations to persist, and, when will you replace them with a philosophy worthy of the excellence you aspire to?

## Parting Thought

Earn, deserve, and consistent. Fault, blame, excuse, and mediocre. You're now on your way to narrowing your focus on specific behaviors, mind-sets, and concepts you must weave into your culture as well as weed out to execute MAX acts, attain the ultimate few objectives (TUFs), maximize your own leadership, define your culture, and build a better team. Although these concepts are simple, mastering the inculcation of one and elimination of the other requires hard and diligent work. But let me reiterate it: It's not complicated. You can do it if you quit the cheap chatter about wanting organizational excellence and actually commit to whatever it takes to get it done. Stop the old talk and start the new walk. *See? It's not rocket science!*

## Rocket Science Rant: A Fast 50 Real-World Rules for Success

One spring, I began posting a daily tip on my Twitter account (@DaveAnderson100) with the intent to run them throughout the high school and college graduation seasons, in an effort to toughen up the mind-set of those who were soon to be joining the workplace. The positive feedback I received during those weeks indicated that many readers found the brief real-world rules useful for meeting starters, coaching conversations, and personal growth. Many even created conference room posters with their favorites. Following are 50, fast, real-world rules for success you may be able to use personally and convey to others as you work to get your process, leadership, culture, and team right. You're likely to notice some of the key points in the previous chapters are summarized nicely within these 50 rules. They will not appeal to the sensitive types, but if you've made it this far in the book, I believe that will not be an issue for you.

1. Get clear about what you want. A narrow focus sharpens discipline and drive; a scattered one diminishes potential.

2. You are entitled to what you acquire through merit, what you have qualified for, and what you are worthy of. Don't expect more.

3. Your diploma is not a license to stop learning. To lead well and earn well, you must continue to learn well.

4. Leadership is about performance, not position. It is a choice you make, not a place at the table where you sit.

5. A problem is something you can solve. A fact of life you must learn to work around. Know the difference.

6. Life rewards action, not knowledge. You won't progress until you get off your knowledge and do something.

7. Accepting blame that is yours while deflecting credit that is not builds trust and draws others to you.

8. Pointing out problems may get you noticed, but solving them gets you into leadership.

9. Don't get so destination focused that you don't enjoy the journey. Make each day a masterpiece.

10. In a world of takers, it's a cinch to stand out by adding value to others and putting them first.

11. Yesterday ended last night. Come to work and prove yourself over again each day.

12. A key to promotion is developing the skills and mind-set of the next position *before* you're in it.

13. Earn influence by promising less, and doing more; giving more, and taking less; and saying less, and listening more.

14. Expect to be measured by results. Efforts are appreciated but results rule.

15. It's better to be a loser than a quitter. Losers can rebound. Quitters simply give up.

16. In a world addicted to blame, you'll find it easy to stand out by simply accepting responsibility.

17. The worst job is to have no job. Don't let "I'm overqualified" become a convenient cover for sloth.

18. *How* you do what you do says more about you than *what* you do. Whatever you do, do with excellence.

19. When leaving the training ground for a battleground, you must turn your stroll into a trot.

20. Don't stop learning! Formal education earned your degree; self-education can earn your fortune.

21. Envy is a distraction. Blame is the antifocus. Excuses are the DNA of underachievers. Avoid them.

22. Executing your job description is not heroic; it's baseline. Going beyond what's required earns acclaim.

23. Credentials buy you only temporary credibility. Results make you credible.

24. Wisdom doesn't enter the head through an open mouth.

25. Ambition is an additive, not a substitute, for character and competence.

26. It's not crowded at the top; it's crowded at the bottom. Go the second mile, and you often go alone.

27. Workplaces don't hand out participation trophies. Expect only what you earn and deserve.

(*continued*)

*(continued)*

28. You're not all that special or unique; you're one of many. To stand out, you must step up.

29. You cannot envy your way into prosperity.

30. Respect is earned, not demanded.

31. You won't accidentally succeed or fail. Neither just happens. Your decisions set you up for one or the other.

32. Develop discipline. It is consistency's fuel, character's ally, and a separator between the good and great.

33. Focus. A scattered focus sabotages success. Like a dog chasing five rabbits, you'll end up drained and with none.

34. Many who want what the successful have are not willing to do what they've done: read books, take risks, develop discipline, and work hard.

35. Formerly, you followed the herd. Now, get out in front, pursue your passion, and leave footprints.

36. When you're late to work, the five minutes is bad enough. What's worse is that you fail to keep your word.

37. It'll be great to change the world, but first, change your address. Part of growing up is moving out of Momma's house.

38. Many people have what you don't have, because they've done what you haven't done. Don't envy them—emulate them.

39. The world is not obligated to make you happy. Attitude, not conditions, governs contentment.

40. The world isn't fair and never has been, nor will it ever be. Stop whining and deal with it.

41. When things are tough, don't think you can wish your way out, whine your way out, or wait your way out. Get off your rear end and work your way out.

42. The easy wins don't help you in the long run. It's the struggles that make you stronger.

43. Strength of character is forged in the pit, not in a hammock.

44. If something is important to you you'll find a way, if it's not you'll find an excuse.

45. When you start to expect something for nothing, you start to become good for nothing.

46. Fairness doesn't mean sameness; fairness means justice. Justice means you get what you earn and deserve.

47. You think you're unique and special? So do the people you work with. Don't make it all about you.

48. You're not the center of the universe. That job has already been taken.

49. When you choose a behavior, you also choose the consequences for that behavior. You're not a victim.

50. Never complain about the money you don't make from the work you will not do.

The preceding fast, 50, real-world rules for success could easily become a fatiguing 500, but we'll stop here because the message is clear. These concepts reinforce numerous "earn and deserve," "take responsibility," and "stop making excuses for execution failure" themes presented throughout this book. To clarify in your mind what a portrait of excellent culture looks like, review the fast 50 from time to time, and refer to the weave-in and weed-out list often. Here's where we're at so far:

**Words to Weave In:**
- Earn: to acquire through merit.
- Deserve: to be worthy of, to qualify for.
- Consistent: constantly adhering to the same principles.
- Lead: to go in front, to show the way.

**Words to Weed Out:**
- Fault: responsibility for failure.
- Blame: to assign responsibility for failure.
- Excuse: a plea offered to excuse a fault or failure.
- Mediocre: average, ordinary, not outstanding.

We still have a ways to go in getting the culture right. Next up are three great words to add to the weave-in side.

# CHAPTER 31

# Weave in Catalyst, Responsible, and Lead

## The Challenge

Too many leaders seem to believe that eventually, a strong culture will take care of itself. They believe that after they've paid their dues and built the right foundation, they can hit the snooze button and see excellence continue ad infinitum. Where they once were proactive shapers of culture, they became passive maintainers of an enterprise in decline. By wrongly thinking culture was a to do item they could cross off a list and declare as "finished," they rendered their own leadership impact as "finished" instead.

## A One-Word Leadership Job Description

In our quest to keep things simple, let me suggest my favorite one-word job description of a leader: catalyst. Here's how I see a catalyst: a thing or person that makes something happen.

It's safe to assume that thinking like a catalyst precedes acting like one. Thus, here's a quick test to evaluate your catalytic mind-set in creating culture, execution, and results. Note how many of these questions, or versions of these questions, you ask yourself as you begin work each day:

- "What can I get started today?"
- "Whom can I get started today?"
- "Whom can I leave better than I find today?"
- "How can I lead by example today?"
- "What can I do to make a difference today?"

In a culture where rhythm of accountability meetings (RAMs) are consistent, master the art of execution (MAX) acts are meaningful, MAX boards are compelling, pruning is consistent, and the ultimate few objectives (TUFs) are attained, the leaders must assume a daily catalytic role.

It's important to also note what wasn't chosen as a simple leadership job description yet is too prevalent in many once-robust cultures:

- Going to work to wait for something to happen, watch something happen, or stare bewildered out the window at day's end and wonder, "What happened?"
- Asking passive questions, such as "I wonder what kind of day we'll have today?," "I wonder how much money we'll make today?," or "I wonder what the team will produce today?"

In high-performance cultures, the leaders assume the role of a catalyst daily, not just when time's running out, when a crisis hits, or when they're backed into a corner and trapped like a rat. Rather, they understand that to get themselves, the process, the culture, and the team right, they must serve as catalysts daily—diligently shaping the culture and energizing their team. And every day means every day (EDMED)!

Another key word, mind-set, and concept that must be woven into a cultural foundation is that of being responsible. *Responsible* is defined as "chargeable with being the author, cause, or occasion of something" (*Dictionary.com*, n.d.).

Perhaps Rudy Giuliani described the essence of responsibility best when during an interview, he identified his philosophy as mayor of New York: "I don't deserve the credit for all that goes right during my term, nor do I deserve the blame for all that goes wrong. But I am still responsible for the results of my office."

Taking responsibility means focusing on what you can control (your daily decisions), not whining about conditions you cannot affect. Leaders who take responsibility teach their people to do likewise. Similarly, leaders who make excuses give their people a permission slip to become victims and rationalize away their lack of greater success.

In a world where blame is pervasive, taking responsibility is a sure way to stand out, earn buy-in, build self-esteem, and build a culture that makes mastering the art of execution possible.

## Parting Thought

It may be helpful at this point to revisit the definition of *leadership* as presented in Part Two, "Get the Leaders Right!": "a position of going in front and showing the way." To those who prefer passivity and blame to leading like a catalyst and taking responsibility, the following friendly warning will be unsettling: The number one cultural threat to any organization doesn't come from the outside but from within. It comes from its own leaders who don't lead and fail to take responsibility for their results. *See? It's not rocket science!*

# 32

# Entitled Out, Tough-Minded In

### The Challenge

Because success can drain urgency, levels of personal and cultural entitlement tend to soar in the good times. Entitlement is a cultural infection that's very difficult to get rid of. It requires redefining expectations, strengthened accountability, consequences for failure, and a return to *earn and deserve* principles within the organization. The weed-out, weave-in words in this chapter are connected to a degree, because without tough-minded leadership and principles, entitlement abounds.

### You Owe Me!

Being entitled is defined as believing you are owed special rewards, privileges, or treatment. The problem arises when people aren't given what they feel they have coming; they have neither earned nor deserved it. Some examples of entitlement are as follows:

- People expect an end-of-the-year raise because it's the end of the year, not because they earned or deserve it.

**161**

- People expect a Thanksgiving turkey every year because you gave it to them once and then listened to complaints about the brand you chose.
- People expect a promotion because they've been there the longest, not because they're the best person for the job.
- The company buys lunch for the team every Friday, and soon they begin to gripe about the free lunch you're giving them: "Pizza again?" "Sandwiches again?" "Why can't we ever get Swiss cheese with our burgers?"
- A poor performer feels entitled to extra help, perks, or attention because he's struggling, not because he's performed in a manner worthy of additional company resources being invested in him.
- People expect their tenure, experience, or credentials to substitute for results; they believe yesteryear's heroics entitle them to a free pass to slack in the present.

With a rise of entitlement in society, you can expect to see more entitlement in businesses, and in households (with entitled kids), because trends in these arenas tend to follow trends in society in general. You can also rest assured that nothing welcomes entitlement into your culture faster than a lack of accountability. On the other hand, it's tougher for people to become entitled when they are held accountable for results and have become accustomed to expecting only what they've earned and deserve.

Often when I rail against entitlement in a seminar, someone will ask me, "Aren't we entitled to something in the workplace?" The answer is, absolutely: all you've earned and deserved, that which you've acquired through merit, what you're worthy of, or what you have qualified for. All perks over and above that are gifts. People should be grateful for them but should understand that they don't have them coming.

In *Up Your Business!* (John Wiley & Sons 2007), I included an entire chapter on how to move a person or an entire organization from entitlement to merit—from thinking they're owed it to expecting only what they've earned and deserve. To summarize the chapter in one idea, the remedy is pressure to perform. This includes clear and high expectations, honest feedback on performance, and accountability for results. In other words, becoming more tough-minded as a leader.

The word *tough-minded* is defined as "strong-willed; vigorous; not easily swayed" (*Dictionary.com*, n.d.). This definition embodies the makeup of high-accountability leaders and strong cultures. Notice that according to the definition, being tough-minded has nothing to do with being rude, being abusive, getting personal, bullying, shouting, or using profanity. In fact, you can be tough-minded in a calm, measured, respectful voice and get your point across far more effectively. In a sense, being tough-minded means you have decided to stand for something to establish your credibility, protect your culture, and execute without excuses. You have also decided what you will not fall for, or settle for, in pursuit of those endeavors:

- You hold everyone accountable for living the core values, including even the high-performing toxic achiever who is prone to be selfish or take shortcuts.
- You apply consequences when necessary for missed performance objectives.
- You hire slowly and strategically, even when you have pressing shortages. You don't flinch, lower the bar, or bring someone on board who will inflict continual damage to the culture and team morale.
- You terminate the nonperformer, even when there's no one readily available to replace him or her, because you understand that it's better to be strategically short staffed than foolishly filled up.
- You routinely make decisions that are hard but right.
- You raise others to reach your expected performance bar; you don't drop the bar to accommodate someone else's comfort zone, character, or competence.

## Parting Thought

Cultures are weakened by complacency, devastated by inconsistency, and destroyed by entitlement. Getting rid of entitlement is a painful process, which is a powerful incentive for not letting it drop anchor in your culture in the first place. Followers may not always like or appreciate you when you demonstrate tough-mindedness, but they are certainly more apt to respect you. Preventing or reversing entitlement and demonstrating tough-mindedness requires the fortitude to do what may be unpopular, costly, or difficult but what also happens to be right. It's not always easy, but nor is it complex. It requires common sense and a stiff spine, not advanced degrees or Einstein's intelligence. *See? It's not rocket science!*

# 33

# Sloth Out, Loyal In

## The Challenge

Leaders commonly mistake someone who works a lot of hours for some one who has a great work ethic. In reality, the person doesn't put much into the hours he or she is at work because sloth has taken hold of his or her life. At the same time, leaders wrongly designate one as being loyal simply because he or she has been on the job for a number of years without enough regard for the actual performance he or she has put into the years. By failing to face reality about people, mediocrity is tolerated too long, inflicting ongoing damage to team culture, chemistry, morale, momentum, and results.

## Sloth Looks Like It Sounds

If there were ever a word that looks in practice like it sounds when you say it, *sloth* is it. *Sloth* is defined as "habitual disinclination to exertion; indolence; laziness" (*Dictionary.com*, n.d.). Sadly, sloth has become a cultural reality in nations, where governments increasingly take more from those who work and give it to those who won't; in families, where entitled and lazy kids emulate Peter Pan and never grow up or leave their parents' nest; and in sports, where even the lazy, disrespectful

**165**

kids have accumulated shelves of worthless participation trophies and ribbons simply for showing up—not for working hard and standing out. Sloth is the natural assassin of consistent execution, and it shows its ugly face in many ways throughout a workplace:

- Employees are passive throughout the day, waiting for something to happen rather than initiating action that could change the course of their day, week, month, or life.
- Workers expect to be rewarded or promoted for baseline performances, rather than for extending themselves and doing more than is required.
- Associates want to be acclaimed, measured, and rewarded more for the hours they put in than by the quality of work they put into the hours.
- Teammates are selfish and won't go out of their way to help another unless there's something in it for them.
- People easily give up on a day, week, or month when things get tough. Their lack of drive and dreams enables sloth and permits it to dominate their lives.
- Too-generous compensation programs reward mediocrity, creating a stimulus program for non-performers and thus, abet sloth.
- Tenure becomes a license for laziness as employees expect their seniority, experience, or track record to substitute for current results.

As cultural diseases, such as entitlement and sloth, pervade more and more organizations, it's no wonder why it has never been easier to stand out in your job. Simply executing daily master the art of execution (MAX) acts will get you noticed. Going far above and beyond expectations, and doing so consistently, can launch you into legendary status.

The key to weeding sloth out of your culture is similar to what's necessary to reverse entitlement. To do so, the following principles prevail:

- Define clear and high expectations.
- Give fast, honest feedback on results.
- Hold rhythm of accountability meetings (RAMs) every day; every day means every day (EDMED).

- Attach accountability consequences for failed performances.
- Continue to prune what is less than optimal: realign, revitalize, or remove.
- Reinforce the concepts of earn and deserve at the bedrock of your culture.

Is it possible for a loyal employee to demonstrate sloth? It all depends on whether you rightly define *loyal*. If you define *loyal* as being similar to seniority or tenure, then absolutely it is possible. If you define *loyal* as it should be defined, you'll find it's totally incompatible with sloth.

The word *loyal* is defined as being faithful to one's duties or obligations. Notice there is nothing in the definition relating to how long someone has been with a company. Although years put in may signify seniority or tenure, they do not automatically mean the long-term employee has been loyal unless he or she is currently faithful to his or her duties and obligations.

Consider these thoughts on the true concept of loyalty, and assess your team members to determine whether those whom you call loyal because they've been with you for many years still qualify for this designation when assessed by the word's proper meaning (perhaps they have succumbed to sloth or mediocrity):

- As with work ethic, loyalty is more about what someone puts into the time than the time someone puts into an organization (quality over quantity).
- In the simplest terms, loyalty is performance. It's possible for a long-term employee to have stopped performing years ago but wrongly to be considered loyal because of a faulty understanding of what being loyal means. Frankly, there's nothing more disloyal than failing to perform well while continuing to collect a paycheck.
- Since tenure can become a license for laziness, oftentimes long-time employees take their jobs for granted, thinking they have paid their dues and shouldn't have to work as hard as when they were first starting with your organization.
- If years of service are your primary criteria for labeling someone as being loyal or not, then the brand-new, high-performing employee

couldn't be considered loyal because he or she hasn't been with you very long (a potentially ridiculous characterization of that person).

- If someone has been with you a long time and still is faithful to his or her duties or obligations, that person is your A player; it just doesn't get much better than that. This person should be a priority, and he or she deserves your utmost appreciation, support, and respect.

If you have to choose between performance and old-time's-sake sentimentalism, you owe it to the culture, your brand, the customer experience, your personal credibility, the company morale, and the rest of the team to opt for performance and insist on a standard where everyone understands that yesterday ended last night and that he or she is expected to bring the best again today—regardless of position, past accomplishments, or years of service.

High-performance cultures understand the true definition of loyalty, establish that standard, and consistently hold all team members accountable for delivering the performance that makes them worthy of being called loyal teammates and employees.

## Parting Thought

If you believe I'm being too hard on the nonperforming or tenured employees by declaring they're not loyal, consider this: Would you call a husband loyal because he's been married to the same woman for 40 years, despite the fact that during those years he was disrespectful, was abusive, and had extramarital affairs? Of course not! You'd probably call him a scoundrel. After all, it wouldn't be the amount of time he put into his marriage that designated him as loyal or not but the unacceptable behaviors he had put into the time. *See? It's not rocket science!*

*Special Note:* My blog on LearnToLead.com has an ongoing series that presents words to weave in, and weed out of, your culture. To expand your perspective on this essential cultural duty, check in there to see words and concepts addressed, such as passion, apathy, maintain, discipline, wise, and foolish.

## Rocket Science Rant: Of Course You're Complacent!

I've rarely met anyone who considered himself or herself complacent, most likely because people have no idea what the word really means. In many cases, they wrongly think it means lazy, slothful, or lethargic. On the other hand, most folks are pretty good at pointing out how another person, department, or competitor is complacent, again demonstrating ignorance of how this tricky word is defined. Years ago in a seminar, I began to explain how complacency affects successful organizations. Suddenly, a business owner in the room raised his hand and told me that it wasn't necessary for me to talk to his team about the dangers of complacency because in his business they had been very successful (yes, occasionally someone attending one of my presentations will open his or her mouth only to have stupid sounds fall out of it). I suggested to the gentleman that he should perhaps pay especially close attention to my words on complacency, because little confesses the fact you are complacent faster than believing it's not problem for you.

*Complacent* is about being calmly content or smugly self-satisfied, which is quite different than being lazy as you'll see in the next point:

1. Once you grasp the true meaning of complacency, it is far easier to spot it in yourself. For starters, you'll realize that complacency isn't so much about the long days you put in on the job as whether you execute the right activities during those long days. You can work 80 hours per week yet be so calmly content with your results that you've stopped training, recruiting, holding people accountable, and more.

2. Successful people and organizations are the most vulnerable targets for complacency. After all, if a business is drowning and gasping for air, it's safe to say the people there are not smugly self-satisfied at the moment. On the other hand, when business is great, and all the seas appear calm, it's easy to become calmly content and abandon many of the vital disciplines, such as MAX acts, rhythm of accountability meetings (RAMs), or proactive pruning, that made you successful in the first place.

3. Complacency is so pervasive that everyone reading these words, including the author writing them, is complacent at

(continued)

*(continued)*

this moment in some area of life: physically, spiritually, mentally, emotionally, with work disciplines, or others. No one is 100 percent, fully *on* in all of life's vital arenas simultaneously. It's humbling to acknowledge that complacency is everyone's problem and that *everyone* includes you and me.

4. Complacency is a threat that never goes away, and as imperfect human beings, we can expect to fall off track in various areas of our life from time to time and become complacent. However, as our awareness of complacency improves, we should expect to get off track less often and to recognize our complacency faster and make quicker course corrections. These two actions will help us shape a culture that greatly outperforms the clueless souls who don't even know what the word *complacent* means and believe it is someone else's problem.

5. Because your biggest vulnerabilities are those you're unaware of, by increasing your own and your team's awareness of what complacency is, you can protect your culture and improve results both personally and as an organization.

Complacent leaders create complacent cultures and followers. If your organization is complacent, it's because you've become complacent. Face it and fix it; otherwise, you're apt to skip merrily down the yellow brick road, smack into a wall of irrelevance.

# Part Three Summary

This chapter has covered immense ground in an effort to help you build a culture that does the following:

- Attracts, develops, and retains great people.
- Fully supports all aspects of the master the art of execution (MAX) process.
- Builds long-term vitality into your organization by firming its foundation, committing to essential cultural fundamentals, and dismissing misguided pursuit of quick fixes to improve results.

To help you accomplish these objectives, you've been equipped with:

- Indisputable awareness that to improve your business, "It's the culture, stupid!"
- The knowledge and responsibility that cultural health is a primary leadership responsibility and that ultimately your culture is in your image.
- An outline of the five cultural pillars you must continue to strengthen to support MAX and the ultimate few objectives (TUFs) fully: core values, mission, performance standards, core competencies, and people.
- A strong reminder that culture, like a garden, is never done—if you don't shape it in your image, society and its accompanying trends, such as entitlement and an absence of absolutes, will do the job for you.

- A blueprint of words, concepts, and mind-sets you must continuously weave into your culture, as well as those you must diligently work to weed out.

Perhaps the key word in this summary thus far lies in the last sentence: diligently. *Diligent* means "done or pursued with persevering attention; painstaking" (*Dictionary.com*, n.d.). Diligence is not an academic or particularly complicated concept, but it requires enormous amounts of energy, focus, dedication, and commitment.

Because I've concluded the final chapters of "Get the Culture Right!" with weave-in words, and weed-out words, it seems reasonable that I'll finish the summary with one last word in each column: interest and commit.

Interest: "The feeling of a person whose attention, concern, or curiosity is particularly engaged by something" (*Dictionary.com*, n.d.).

Commit: "To pledge (oneself) to a position on an issue or question; express (one's intention, feeling, etc.)" (*Dictionary.com*, n.d.).

You have a choice to make before moving forward to get your culture right: Are you interested in the work required to build a high-performance culture, or are you truly committed to it? Are you "curious" about what it might be like to become great as a leader and an organization, or are you willing to pledge yourself to that endeavor? Pledging oneself infers you'll pay a price, and common sense suggests it is not a one-time, lump sum payment but will be an installment plan with a term that lasts as long as you're in the arena.

By the way, you don't have to answer the interest versus committed challenge verbally; your actions will tell the story. People will be able to determine your choice by watching you, regardless of which it is.

So, the ball's in your court. Making the right decision doesn't involve calculus or chemistry. It does require heart. Interested or committed? You can pick only one. *See? It's not rocket science!*

# PART FOUR

# GET THE TEAM RIGHT!

Regardless of how great you are as a leader, there's only so much you can accomplish alone with your own talent, energy, skills, and work ethic. If your goals are small, you probably can accomplish them alone. Even a klutz of a leader can bumble around by himself or herself and manage to climb atop a molehill. But if you want to do something significant, if you want to climb Mt. Everest, you had better bring some people with you; and they need to be the right people. The wrong team can turn your journey to greater heights into a nightmare.

If you've already begun putting into practice the strategies learned in "Get the Process Right!," "Get the Leader Right!," and "Get the Culture Right!," you should be spending more productive time with your team. You should be keeping team members focused on master the art of execution (MAX) acts and the ultimate few objectives (TUFs), holding them increasingly accountable with the MAX board and rhythm of accountability meetings (RAMs), building a stronger culture for them to thrive in, and seeing better results in return for your efforts. "Get the Team Right!," the final strategy for mastering the art of execution, will leverage the foundation you've built thus far by providing insights on how to better assess, develop, engage, and use the talents of people, as well as how to retain your human capital.

Many leaders have worked hard to develop their people but haven't yet developed the leadership skills, built the right culture, or installed an effective execution process like MAX to realize their potential in that regard. As you apply what you have learned to affect those aspects of your business positively, "Get the Team Right!" will prove to be the most fun and rewarding of the four strategies. In fact, if helping people grow and seeing the difference you make in their lives doesn't serve as the ultimate leadership high for you, then you should reevaluate your fitness for leadership; followers deserve a leader who values them enough to make effective people work a priority.

# CHAPTER 34

# How to Find the Great People You're Looking For!

## The Challenge

One of the most persistent questions leaders ask me at seminars is "How and where do I find great people?" The most obvious but overlooked answer to this question is to start with those you have. If you haven't done what is necessary to develop the people already on your team, it is irresponsible to dismiss their potential, discard them, hire new people, and then subject them to the same neglect. Your challenge is to ensure you have the mind-set and disciplines in place to bring out the best in those already on your team. Following is a 10-point checklist to help ensure that you do. The good news is that if you have already started implementing strategies from prior chapters, you will have a head start in many of these areas. Use these 10 points as a review to gauge how much action you have taken in these areas.

## Ten-Point People Development Checklist

1. *Set clear performance standards for them.* This point should be abundantly clear by now. Quality employees will strive hard to hit your standards if you're clear about what they are in the first place. One of your first responsibilities as a leader is to make it precisely clear what you expect from each team member. If you have not yet identified his or her master the art of execution (MAX) acts, and presented them on personalized success profiles (PSPs), then you should start there.

2. *Make certain they understand your mission and core values.* These aspects of organizational culture and clarity serve as a resource to keep them focused on the goals that matter most. Likewise, they act as a filter to help them make decisions, know right from wrong, and take appropriate action in given situations.

3. *Learn their motivational triggers.* As first suggested in "Get the Leaders Right!," you must know people to move people. The only way to truly know them is by investing your time in a relationship with them to determine their strengths, weaknesses, aspirations, and motivational triggers. More on how to do this will be presented in an upcoming chapter on improving employee engagement.

4. *Give them fast, honest, and specific feedback on performance.* As a friendly reminder, feedback eliminates gray areas that cause people to wonder how they are doing or speculate whether anyone even cares. Positive reinforcement will bring closure to the productive things they do and increase the chances they do more of those things. Constructive feedback will confront errant behaviors, give you a chance to redefine what is expected, and make it less likely that they will do the same wrong things again. It is essential that any feedback is given as close after the performance as possible and is specific in both your praise and correction. But remember, until TUFs, MAX acts, core values, and mission are clearly established, you have no basis for intelligent or meaningful feedback.

5. *Hold them accountable for results.* You must care enough to confront them with honest feedback and appropriate consequences, when necessary, to stop or turn around unacceptable

behaviors and production levels and get them back on track. If you are still flinching at the thought of tightening up on accountability, keep this in mind: Accountability is not punishment. Accountability demonstrates that you care and are interested in helping improve a team member's performance.

6. *Consistently train them.* Your job is to take the human capital on your team and make it more valuable through training. This means you must provide the time, tools, and structure for team members to upgrade their skills, habits, and attitude consistently. If the cost of training gives you pause, consider the cost of having people who remain ignorant and unproductive because you don't train them. If you are not an effective trainer, or you do not know how to train, you can improve. Attend one of my Train the Trainer workshops at our Elite Center in Los Angeles, and I will coach you personally.

7. *Schedule and conduct one-on-one coaching sessions, and make sure they're developmental rather than punitive.* Although the occasional punitive, one-on-one coaching session may be necessary to address poor performance, one-on-one coaching sessions are intended primarily for drawing out the talent and potential each team member brings to the table. They are an incredible opportunity for you to listen to, coach, reinforce, and challenge each team member to higher performance levels. Prioritize one-on-ones.

8. *Lead by example.* This includes keeping your commitments, living the company core values, putting people work before paperwork, having a personal growth program, and placing the team's welfare ahead of your personal pride, preferences, or agenda.

9. *When they are not performing well, evaluate them with the hope versus wish or three Ts filter.* I presented these filters in the "Get the Leaders Right!" part. They're highly effective.

10. *If after following these strategies, the team member still does not make measurable progress in reasonable time, remove him or her.* Continuing to invest time and resources into a team member who will not, or cannot, grow cheats those on your team who are bringing to the table what it takes to succeed. There comes a time when the removal aspect of pruning is necessary.

Incidentally, if you persistently have high turnover issues in a given department, there is a very good chance that the leader of that department is the primary problem (and this may mean you). If you are that leader's supervisor, make sure you're following the same 10 steps with him or her so that he or she is equipped to perform to your expectations.

## Parting Thought

It may help to remember that when Coach Vince Lombardi took over the Green Bay Packers in 1959, he inherited a team that had suffered through 11 straight losing seasons and had finished the 1958 season with a record of 1–10–1. He turned the team into winners the very next year, largely with the same men (there was no free agency in 1959). Under his leadership, seven of the players on the 1958 team went to the Hall of Fame, including Bart Starr, Paul Hornung, and Jim Taylor—all of whom were warming the bench under prior coach Scooter McLean. Eleven of the players on the 1958 team later went on to become All-Pros. Where do you find great people? Start with those you have. *See? It's not rocket science!*

# *Like* is Never Enough!

## The Challenge

A common mistake made when hiring is bringing someone on board primarily because the interviewers like him or her, based on their own preferences, stereotypes, or personal biases. Although liking a potential team member is a plus, and can improve chemistry, likability is not an accurate indicator of character or competence. In fact, most of us have seen employees who were once likeable become far less so as we discovered flaws in their behaviors we should have uncovered during the interview process. Although my books *TKO Hiring!* and *Up Your Business!* (John Wiley & Sons 2007) address recruiting, interviewing, and hiring in greater depth, I will review a couple of basic premises for getting the people right in this chapter.

## Don't Get Emotional!

Hiring experts have long asserted that the number one cause of hiring errors is making emotional decisions during the interview process.

If you have ever been caught up in the emotional decision trap, some of the following may sound familiar:

- Early on in the interview you decide you like someone based on your personal biases or stereotypes, or his or her appearance and personality.
- At the "I really like this guy" moment, you begin to lose your objectivity and cease to assess the candidate as rigorously.
- After losing your objectivity you are no longer tough in your assessment of this person and begin looking for a way to include him or her on the team (exaggerating the candidate's strengths and minimizing his or her weaknesses).
- The interview has now devolved from a fact-finding proposition to a casual conversation, a good-ol'-boy get-acquainted session, or worse, a sales pitch.

As human beings, we are easily swayed by the factors outlined in the first point, causing us to give an unqualified and unfit candidate far too much benefit of the doubt. This is why using a preemployment assessment can help you tremendously. The right assessment will dig beneath the veneer of a candidate's best interview behavior and detect areas for concern that you should investigate further through a second interview, or, you may find cause to eliminate the person from consideration altogether, saving you untold dollars, momentum, morale, culture damage, and personal credibility. Although assessments aren't a perfect solution for eliminating hiring errors, they are a key ally in helping you fire the wrong person before you hire him or her. Over the years, I've heard confessions from numerous managers who went against what the assessment recommended, hired the person anyway, and soon lived to regret it.

## Let the Assessment Assess!

We are especially prone to developing blind spots concerning a candidate's weaknesses when recruiting people into our business whom we know or whom we think we know. This may be a friend, a friend of a friend, an associate you do business with, or someone you are personally recruiting. I fell into this trap years ago when recruiting

"Ed" from our bank and compounded the error by ignoring the frightening score Ed made on our namesake Anderson Pre-Employment Profile because I "liked" Ed. I mistakenly assumed that I knew him better than our assessment did; after all, I had done business with him for three years at the bank where I first met him. The two biggest concerns our assessment flagged after evaluating Ed's 24 personality traits were:

- He would be uncoachable.
- He would be selfish and unconcerned about the welfare of other teammates—a law unto himself.

In other words, we could expect Ed to be late to work, not to help others out, and never to take ownership of the company's mission or his own mistakes. Ultimately, he'd be a lone wolf hired gun who looked at us as just a job rather than a career and would probably keep looking for something better—all while he was collecting our paychecks.

Considering our five core values I presented in "Get the Culture Right!" and how serious we are about team members living up to them, Ed's assessment should have stopped me cold in my quest to hire him.

The Ed I did business with at our bank and thought I'd known for the past three years (and who did great during the interview process) proved every dire prediction of the Anderson Pre-Employment Profile true quickly after we hired him. To make a long story short, he violated our integrity, teamwork, urgency, and attention-to-detail values by being late three times to work in one week and I fired him. I haven't second-guessed my namesake preemployment profile since I let Ed go.

I still like Ed. He's a nice guy with a professional appearance and well-spoken manner. He was competent in his work. He simply wasn't a good fit for our culture, proving once again the words I have preached for years but had to eat one last time: *Like is not enough.*

**Note:** If you'd like to protect your organization from hiring errors, visit www.learntolead.com, and read up on the Anderson Profiles. They are based on over 40 years of Winslow research and expertise.

## Parting Thought

Interviews should be tough and fact-finding expeditions rather than happy hot-tub talk sessions. You need prestructured questions to ask that help determine character and competence. Speak less and listen more. Dig deep into a candidate's answers to weed out exaggeration. Look more for past accomplishments than past experience. Remember what you're opening to injury with just a single bad hire: momentum, morale, culture, brand strength, production levels, your credibility, and more. This is why the overriding objective of an interview is to eliminate the candidate, not to find ways to include him or her. If you cannot eliminate the person, you may be onto something very positive for your organization. Follow your head, not your heart. *See? It's not rocket science!*

# CHAPTER 36

# You Can't Make People What They Are Not!

## The Challenge

Many leaders, in their quest to elevate a nonperformer heroically into a contributor, overlook one of the first rules of people development: *I can help make you more of what you are, but I can't make you something you're not.* There are key and critical success factors you cannot change about others, nor can you teach them to others. If you have people on your team lacking these traits, then the time, training, and motivational efforts you invest in them will bring little or no return. Thus, it's essential that you hire people who bring these assets to the table. This chapter will outline six such traits to look for when hiring someone into your organization. These traits are also a useful template to assess the growth potential of those already on your team.

## Good News and Not-So-Good News

First, the good news: There are two key things you can teach others (skills and knowledge). In fact, the definition of *teach* is "to impart knowledge of or skill in" (*Dictionary.com*, n.d.). You can teach technical skills, closing skills, knowledge of a product or system, and the like.

Now, the not-so-good-news: The following six traits are factors you cannot change about someone, put inside someone, or even effectively teach to someone. To maximize performance, these traits must be hired in and then developed with consistent coaching and within a strong culture.

1. *Talent.* Defined as "a special or natural ability or aptitude" (*Dictionary.com*, n.d.).

    The hard truth is that, regardless of how hard you try, you cannot teach a natural ability; you must hire it in and develop it. In fact, you can't make yourself talented either, which is why anyone wanting to excel must pursue the talents he or she has, not the talents he or she wants. Without question, everyone has a talent for something; what's essential is that your team members have the talents to accomplish what you are paying them to do.

    Although it's also true that talent is never a guarantee of performance, it does provide a great head start toward excellence. In fact, excellence is impossible without talent. This is why training untalented people longer, harder, and faster won't make them great in positions where they have no natural ability or aptitude. The best you can hope for is to make them less bad. Not very inspiring, is it?

2. *Drive.* Drive is rooted in having an innate biologically determined urge to attain a goal or satisfy a need.

    You cannot teach what is innate, nor can you make anyone driven. Drive is an inside job. In fact, drive is like talent in that you cannot put inside of someone what's not there; you can only draw out what exists. You may certainly be able to change someone's drive level temporarily with a deadline, incentive, or threat, but without genuine internal drive, as soon as the external stimulus disappears, so does the drive. Drive is stirred up by the *why*, the red belt hunger that causes one to do what is necessary to satisfy personal reasons for wanting success.

3. *Attitude.* Attitude is a settled way of thinking that's reflected in one's behavior; one's prevailing outlook on life.

   Most would admit it's hard enough to change your own feelings and thus, the chances of changing someone else's prevailing outlook on life are remote. Of course, you can temporarily alter others' mood based on how you treat them, but their natural attitude—good or bad—will eventually wiggle its way back out.

   At the end of the day, each of us is responsible for choosing our own attitude. Although we can't choose what happens to us, we do have the power to choose how we respond, and negative (*can't do*) people have a long history of making the wrong choices in the attitude arena. Can someone change? Yes! Can you change him or her in this regard? No!

4. *Character.* Defined as "the aggregate of features and traits that form the individual nature of some person or thing" (*Dictionary .com*, n.d.).

   Chances are good that we have all tried to influence someone's character with a good example, words of moral wisdom, or a diatribe on ethics. But despite heroic efforts, we mortal beings remain incapable of changing the individual nature of other human beings. Again, the question is, Can they change? Yes! Can you change them in regard to character? Absolutely not! Much like attitude, character results from the choices people make and the values they embrace. You can't make those choices for them.

5. *Energy.* Energy is about having the strength and vitality for sustained mental or physical activity.

   Some folks have strong internal drive, and they start the day with a flash, but run out of gas by midafternoon or become overwhelmed when required to demonstrate the mental vitality to juggle multiple tasks simultaneously. Neither you, nor I, can teach anyone the strength and vitality required for sustained physical and mental activity. Although external forces can affect energy (like drive), they are not sustainable.

6. *Passion.* Passion concerns excitement or enthusiasm about something, or about doing something.

   Neither drive nor energy compensates for a lack of passion. Many people have high drive and energy levels but lack excitement or enthusiasm for what they do. As a result, they often feel frustrated and misemployed. Passion, like drive, can lie dormant in someone and may be aroused by a compelling vision, need, or cause. You can stir it up, but you cannot force it down.

A leader's obligation is to create the conditions to arouse that passion in others through meaningful work and with a compelling purpose. However, pep talks and positive reinforcement don't substitute for the internal passion someone must have to excel through the many ups and downs in a particular position sustainably. When all is said and done, you cannot make anyone passionate about what he or she is doing.

It's also important to note that you can make someone temporarily driven or energized by employing tactics such as incentives or threats, but, it's exhausting to have to manage people in this manner—to bribe them or threaten them to bring them to life. Besides, if external forces are required to get someone moving, as soon as those external forces go away, so does the movement.

The most effective way to assess whether a potential employee has these six traits is the interview. Rigorous, in-depth interviews, anchored in highly effective questions, will help uncover the existence—or lack—of these traits within someone. After all, when you dig into a job candidate's life, these six factors will either show up or not. Success leaves clues and so does failure. Although you can't expect to find perfect people, anyone can get off track from time to time in these vital areas. These off-track occurrences, however, must be, by far, the exception rather than the rule.

The same reasoning applies when you're evaluating those currently on your team for future performance potential. Knowing that you have a limited ability to affect any current team member without these six traits, you should be able to more accurately assess his or her ability to contribute to your organization in the future.

## Parting Thought

The bottom line is your life and business become easier when you really, *really*, REALLY grasp that some people will not change, no matter what you do. Face it and deal with it. *See? It's not rocket science!*

# 37

# Ten Tips to Retain Talent

## The Challenge

Talent isn't likely to show up at your organization's doorstep fully developed. Although you cannot put into someone what was left out, your job is to do all you can to draw out of someone what is within him or her. Developing and retaining talent are two key aspects of getting the team right. Following is a 10-point checklist to grade your organization in this regard. You will likely notice some recurring themes from earlier chapters throughout the book. They are here again for a reason—they are important. Plus, I don't mind mentioning something 10 times, 10 ways, if one of them gets through and causes you to take action.

## Ten Tips

1. *Hire right*. If you don't hire people with the character and competence to achieve your objectives, they will most likely fail and leave (or they will fail and you'll fire them). By considering hiring as an elimination process, and using strategic

questions to dig into a candidate's life to search for the six key traits listed in the last chapter, you will take huge strides forward in this regard. In addition, you'll save yourself from being duped by the *like* factor during an interview.

2. *Lead by example.* If you are applying what you learned in "Get the Leaders Right!," you should be progressing well in this area. This is a daily discipline, and one poor decision concerning your values or motives can derail the months or years of reputation that you have built. Stay sharp.

3. *Develop the talent in your charge.* If you have good people and you don't consistently train, coach, and mentor them, then you don't deserve them; in fact, you deserve to lose them and in time you will. How consistent are your training disciplines? Whom are you currently mentoring? Do you schedule one-on-one coaching sessions with your team members? Remember: To grow people, you must prioritize people work over the paperwork—the stuff.

4. *Set clear expectations.* Yes, here is this point again. I hope its importance is getting through. If master the art of execution (MAX) is alive and well within your culture, you should be in great shape here with clear ultimate few objectives (TUFs) and MAX acts.

5. *Offer fast, frequent, and honest feedback.* Yep, you knew this had to be within the top 10. Once expectations are set, good performers want to know how they're doing. If they're great, tell them; if they are failing, tell them that, too, and show them how to turn things around. Feedback is the breakfast of champions, and the majority of workers say either they don't get enough of it or when they do get it, it's often too late to make much of a difference. Fast, frequent, honest feedback engages your people, builds performance, and helps retain your talent. If you're using a MAX board, and conducting consistent rhythm of accountability meetings (RAMs), you're well on your way to scoring high here.

6. *Hold them accountable for results.* Lest you believed you had heard the last about holding people accountable, here's another reminder: Don't fall for the politically correct, *hug and burp*

*them* philosophy that people want to be coddled and that they resent accountability. Solid players resent accountability only when you never set clear expectations in the first place. Human beings need the discomfort of accountability to focus, engage, and grow to their potential. If you truly care about your people, you will hold them to a high enough standard to bring out their best. If you believe holding people accountable is harsh, then consider what's truly brutal: letting people fail on your watch because you won't do your job.

7. *Inspire with mission and vision.* This is a cultural issue, and if you've been working on the strategies given in "Get the Culture Right!," you should have momentum here. Frankly, good people don't just want a job; they want a cause. They yearn to be part of something special and to make a difference. Think about it. People quit jobs, but they die for causes because causes engage and inspire them. That being said, it's the leader's job to create and cast a unifying mission and vision that bring a team together and lend more meaning to the workplace.

8. *Empower them.* If your best people don't feel challenged, trusted, or that they're growing into new responsibilities, you are likely to lose them. It's just a matter of time. Empowering people with broadened latitude and discretion to stretch their abilities and make them more valuable is an essential retention tool. By finding ways to make your people less dependent on you, you will elevate their morale and growth. You will also find yourself more effective because you do not have to personally make every decision, solve all the problems, and have every idea.

9. *Engage them.* There's an entire chapter forthcoming on this topic. For now, let me plant the seed in you that happy or satisfied employees aren't necessarily engaged employees, but, engaged employees are far more likely to feel happy and satisfied. As the leader, nothing stimulates engagement more effectively than the strength of your relationship with direct reports.

10. *Reward them fairly.* If you get people cheaply, it normally doesn't take long to discover why. If you pay peanuts, you can expect to get monkeys. Great people have options, and although culture,

team chemistry, and a worthy vision are all significant motivators, no one likes to be undervalued or taken for granted financially. Little will cost you more temporary morale and permanent loss of talent than greed.

## Parting Thought

If you have so-so performers but don't score well in these 10 areas, the other people may not be the problem—you are probably the problem. If you're not aware of these 10 steps for retaining talent, you can hide behind an explanation of ignorance, but if you're aware of them (and now you are) and still neglect them, then what you are doing is just plain stupid! There is no excuse. *See? It's not rocket science!*

# CHAPTER 38

# Fix the Roof While the Sun Is Shining!

## The Challenge

Because prosperity drains urgency, and things naturally wind down rather than up, most leaders won't get serious about finding, developing, or retaining talent, or dealing with deadweight, until something bad happens (the red-ink quarter, an economic downturn, a top performer defects, or some other unforeseen crisis). To strengthen your culture and consistently increase results, you will need to become far more proactive and fix the roof while the sun is shining. And if things have already turned down for you, learn the lessons inherent in your reversal, and resolve to do better going forward.

## JFK Was Right

In his 1962 State of the Union Address, John F. Kennedy declared, "The best time to repair the roof is when the sun is shining" (BrainyQuote, n.d.). His philosophy wasn't intended for organizations per se, but it fits quite well, especially during times of abundance.

Remember: Just like in physics, organizational momentum naturally winds down rather than up unless outside energy is applied. You won't plunge downward when you neglect the right disciplines—you'll slope there. Because of this, you often will not realize you are in decline until it's too late.

If you have momentum, it is easier to steer than to restart, so here are three suggested actions you can take to leverage momentum when you have it:

1. *Redefine performance expectations while things are going well.* There's no better time to redefine performance expectations for the organization overall, and for each team member, than when things are already rolling along. This keeps people sharp, focused, and in a stretch mode. Redefined expectations should meet the following criteria:
   - They are in writing.
   - There are daily activity objectives—master the art of execution (MAX) acts—not just outcome goals—the ultimate few objectives (TUFs).
   - There are consequences for failing to meet a standard.
   - The team standards are introduced to the group as a whole and then gone over one-on-one as you relate each individual's required contribution to the total team effort.
   - The expectations become part of the conversation in meetings, during private coaching sessions, and at performance reviews.

If you are not sure whether your current expectations are clear enough or high enough, they're probably not. Practice presenting new performance expectations in a positive, rather than a highhanded or threatening, manner, with a script similar to this:

> Team, we are in a great position to leverage our current momentum for even greater success. But for us to reach our potential, I know I need to do a better job of defining exactly what I expect from each of you daily, weekly, and monthly going forward. In this meeting I want to give you some clearer targets to shoot for that will get

us on the same page and help you become more successful. If we all step up, we can make something very special happen here this year.

Incidentally, if your performance expectations aren't clear enough, it will be extremely difficult for you to hold anyone accountable because the question becomes "Accountable for what?" This brings us to the next suggested step for how to fix the roof while the sun is shining:

2. *Remove the deadweight.* During tough times, removing dead-weight isn't normally a problem. The temptation during robust business periods is to learn to live with, work around, or rationalize performers operating at levels unworthy of your standards. Deadweight, enabled by a lack of accountability, breaks momentum, lowers morale, hurts the customer experience, and can destroy your personal credibility as a leader. If you have set clear expectations, have consistently invested in the development of a team member, offer honest and fast feedback to eliminate gray areas and blind spots, and still have no grounds for believing tomorrow's performance will be any better than today, then you should apply the three Ts filter to determine your next step. Leadership is about doing what is right. It is about putting what's best for the team overall before your personal likes, preferences, convenience, or comfort zone.

3. *Don't overmanage and underlead.* This point takes us back to what I discussed early in the "Get the Leaders Right!" part. When everything seems to be rocking and under control, it's tempting to disengage and spend less time in the trenches and more in your office (engaging more in paperwork than in people work, substituting rules for relationships, and talking like a leader but acting like an anchor). Continue leading daily by focusing on simple disciplines. Here are quick reminders:

   - *Commit to daily* wanderarounds where you get into the trenches with your people, give feedback, seek out feedback, catch people doing things right, and quickly correct them when they're off track.

- *Schedule one-on-one coaching sessions* with team members so that you formally and systematically grow them to new levels.
- *Take your training program up a notch.* Devise weekly training themes, assign tasks for people to work on in between your training meetings, require action plans from attendees, and then follow up during one-on-ones to help them implement what they committed to do.

## Parting Thought

Do not wait for something bad to happen before you fix, reinforce, or rebuild your roof. Although these steps are basic, they are not necessarily easy. They require hard, smart work. But that's why you make the big bucks. As a leader, if you're not going to get this done, then whose job is it? If you are not going to begin now, then what's your reasoning? The answers are obvious: You are the one, and now is the time. *See? It's not rocket science!*

# 39

# Six Ways to Increase Employee Engagement

## The Challenge

The past few years have brought a stronger awareness of the importance of having engaged employees in the workplace, while definitions as to what it actually means to be engaged are mostly misguided. Popular opinion asserts that happy and satisfied employees should be a priority, and many assume that if employees are happy with their work, and satisfied with their workplace, that their engagement is a given. This assertion is both wrong and reckless.

## Two Truths about Engagement

- Some employees are *happy* to hang out by the water cooler daily for much of the day gossiping, snacking, and working hard at looking busy. Could you honestly call these happy folks engaged?

- Some team members are *satisfied* to do just enough to get by each day, just enough to get paid, and just enough not to get fired. These are not the behaviors any rational person would deem as engaged.

The reality is that employee engagement doesn't come from an employee being happy or satisfied; rather, that happiness and satisfaction result from an employee being engaged with his or her work, and at his or her workplace.

To dig deeper into the engagement topic, let's get past the buzzword aspect of *engagement* and examine insights into what it looks like in practice as well as how to create it.

## How to Increase Engagement Effectively

1. *Employee engagement happens when an employee is emotionally invested in the company's goals.* His or her work is not just a means to a paycheck but also a place where he or she finds significant meaning and purpose. Yes, the employee wants to make money, but he or she also wants to make a difference; when engaged, he or she does not feel like just a number, but rather, a part of something special. Your ultimate few objectives (TUFs), mission, and core values are a great help in this regard.

2. *The degree to which an employee is emotionally invested in a company's goals will depend largely on the strength of the relationship he or she has with his or her direct supervisor.* It's incumbent on the leader to initiate the relationship with an employee and take the lead to strengthen it over time. To this end, a leader must genuinely prioritize people. Ceasing the habit of overmanaging and underleading will be a giant leap forward to achieve the healthy relationships necessary for strong engagement.

3. *When a leader substitutes rules for relationships, he or she gets rebellion, not engagement.* If you persist in spending more time with stuff than people, you will eventually reap rebellion from among the ranks. Rebellion manifests in many ways, from coming into work late, to doing the bare minimum to get by, to not speaking well of coworkers or the company when away from the job.

4. *Empowering team members with latitude and discretion increases engagement.* Helping your people think and act on their own by

empowering them to make more of their own decisions, solve their own problems, and implement their own ideas builds their self-esteem and allows them to take more ownership in their jobs. Empowering is more than simply telling someone it's okay to do something. It means creating clear expectations for what you expect and helping him or her develop the skills to deliver.

5. *Helping your team members develop a personal growth program improves their level of engagement.* Little creates more goodwill and engagement than when you take a hands-on interest in helping the people on your team grow personally so that they can reach their fullest potential. Helping them define growth objectives and then determining the resources necessary to achieve them not only increases engagement but also builds a higher sense of loyalty to you personally and to the organization.

6. *Learn to motivate each team member as a unique individual, rather than applying assembly line management.* Everyone has different strengths, weaknesses, aspirations, whys, and motivations. When team members believe their boss cares enough to understand them and treat them as the unique entities they are, engagement soars.

## Parting Thought

There's much more to say about employee engagement and dozens of additional strategies and tactics one can use to create it. These points, however, provide both a checklist to evaluate how you're doing as a leader and a blueprint to begin taking more proactive action to maximize engagement in your organization. They will go a long way in determining whether your team members feel like stakeholders or driven stakes. Executing these six points doesn't require a bank loan, an economic upturn, or the collapse of a competitor. They are based on you simply making the right decisions to prioritize people and the relationship you have with them. *See? It's not rocket science!*

CHAPTER 40

# The Staggering Cost of Poor Performance

## The Challenge

In nearly every workshop, I ask the following question: *"How many of you would agree that most organizations tend to keep poor performers too long?"* Every time, hordes of hands shoot up, demonstrating yet again that the largest gap in business or in life is the gap between knowing and doing. Most often we're not held back because we lack knowledge but because we don't do what we know we should.

## Count the Costs . . . If You Dare

Although it's difficult to precisely quantify the cost of just a single poor performer (some researchers have attempted to), I feel safe in asserting that if managers more carefully considered the resulting damage, they would be inclined to more quickly prioritize either getting the person better or getting a better person. You may recognize some of these themes from our chapter regarding the people pillar of culture. Do you know why they are here? Because most likely, the people who came to your mind when you read that chapter are still

**199**

here as well. Here's a quick sampling of what your failure to do your job is costing you and your organization:

- *Lost production.* This factor may be the easiest to quantify, because it is found by comparing the production difference between a top and bottom performer. The fact that this cost is incurred month in and month out causes the penalty for delayed action in turning around or removing poor performers to escalate in a hurry.

- *Broken or lost momentum.* How can one possibly quantify the cost of broken or lost momentum caused by someone who needs continual reprimands, who creates mess after mess, or whose behavior brings about emergencies of the moment that others must stop to solve or repair. To exacerbate this factor, consider that it always hurts more to lose momentum when things are rolling along. Ironically, this is the time a manager is least likely to confront or remove a poor performer. After all, when business is good and all the seas appear calm, complacency entices managers to stay the course and maintain, rather than make the tough decisions they are being paid to execute concerning poor performance.

- *Lower morale.* Most would agree that a poor performer diminishes the collective self-esteem of an entire group. Top performers especially feel at least slightly cheapened and depleted when working with those who don't contribute toward the organization's ultimate few objectives (TUFs), instead making the workplace feel less special.

- *Lost or damaged credibility.* This one really stings, because credibility takes enormous time and effort to build and is even more difficult to regain once you've lost it. It is sad to hear managers boast about how they are "number one," how they have built a "unique place to work," and how "not everyone can be one of us" and then see disillusioned teammates peruse the organization, mumbling: *"'Number one?' 'Unique place to work?' 'Not everyone can be one of us?' Really? And Fred is still here? And Suzy? And Carl? Hmmm, the boss is talking right and walking left again. Does he think we haven't noticed what's really going on here?"* To compound the credibility dilemma, consider this: You will lose the respect of the best when you fail to deal effectively with the worst. Guaranteed.

I do not have the space in this chapter to delve into the additional costs poor performers inflict on your brand, culture, customer experience, training dollars, and labor hours invested (all in a low-return or no-return project). It would be easier if the cost that a single poor performer caused you were a one-time, lump sum payment, but it's not. Rather, poor performers create an ongoing misery on the installment plan that persists in perennially picking your pocket.

The purpose of this chapter is to create a clearer perspective of the staggering costs of poor performance so that you can begin to deal with it faster. The chapter "How to Find the Great People You're Looking For!" dealt with improving the people already on your team. The chapter "A Blueprint for Making the Tough Calls" provided the hope versus wish filter and the three Ts filter for determining pruning strategies for less-than-optimal performers. To round things out, I will end this chapter with eight additional insights concerning your responsibility to deal with poor performance quickly, professionally, and firmly. The first point is a quick reminder:

1. *Hire right!* Here we go again, but you can't escape the reality that a key cause of poor performance is hiring the wrong person to begin with. The fastest way to prevent the presence of future poor performers is to improve your recruiting, interviewing, and assessment strategies dramatically.

2. *Keeping a poor performer simply because you are shorthanded poses the question "What are your plans to create a recruiting process that builds a pipeline of talented people so that you're not held hostage by people who shouldn't even be on your team in the first place?"*

3. *Your solid performers would rather be short-handed and have to work a bit harder temporarily, than have to work harder indefinitely because you keep the wrong people on your payroll, which causes them to do their own share and someone else's.* They would prefer to carry a bigger load personally than their load and the load of someone who shouldn't be on the team in the first place.

4. *A poor performer isn't always a low producer.* He or she could be a top producer with serious character flaws who mocks your values and undermines the performance of the team overall.

5. *The costs you pay in unemployment insurance that results from terminations pale in comparison with the penalties you incur by*

*keeping someone who continues to affect production, momentum, morale, your credibility, the brand, the culture, customer experience, and more.*

6. *A poor-performing manager should be given less rope, and less time to get it together, than a poor-performing subordinate.* The stakes are considerably higher when the leaders are poor performers because of the many others they negatively affect and hold back every day.

7. *If you have a manager who must continually fire poor performers, then he or she is the problem.* He or she most likely is hiring recklessly; hasn't created a high-performing culture where great people are attracted and can prosper; or has failed to set clear expectations, train, or hold accountable the people who are failing.

8. *The role of human resources is to facilitate the removal of poor performers, not to block it.*

## Parting Thought

If you have deadweight in your organization, and you can, but don't, do anything about it, then *you* are the deadweight. Don't shoot the messenger. I'm just trying to be helpful. There's no sense in looking around for a more palatable option. You've met the problem, and it's you. *See? It's not rocket science!*

---

### Rocket Science Rant: You're a Leader, Not a Nanny!

Some managers should wear bonnets and carry diaper bags, because in their management role, they function more as a nanny than as a leader.

I'm taken aback as I visit businesses on consulting missions and see managers nearly begging their people to do their jobs. They sweet-talk, entice, and cajole but rarely ever lay it on the line, follow through with consequences, or care enough to confront their people with tough love. If this describes you, keep this in mind: At the end of the day, your job is not to make people happy—it is to help them get better. Once they get better, they normally become happier. And if improving their skills, sense of purpose, self-esteem, and income doesn't make them happy, then you have the wrong people!

Is it more fun when everyone is happy? Of course it is. Is it necessary, or even possible, to make everyone happy? No. After all, you're a leader, not a clown, diplomat, or therapist. One of the most liberating days of my life was when I gave up trying to make everyone happy, focusing instead on doing what was right for the individual and the organization overall. I started stretching and stopped compromising. I expected greater effort and accepted fewer excuses.

If you truly care about people, you won't be easy on them and watch them fail to reach their potential while you let indifference preside. Instead, you will take actions like the following. Please consider this as a final checklist of sorts, as this book reaches its conclusion.

- Be resolutely clear about what you expect. This should be quite clear by now. If you fail to do this, you fail—period.
- Make certain that what you expect will stretch people and that they cannot accomplish their objectives with a business-as-usual approach.
- Be respectful and constructive with honest feedback. Never make it personal. At the same time, quickly reward people with appropriate praise when they do well.
- Ready for this? Hold them accountable. Has this one gotten through yet? If you want to change a behavior, you've got to change the consequences for that behavior.
- Show them what good performance looks like; don't just tell them.
- Give your people new opportunities. Look for ways to take them out of their comfort zone by broadening their discretion. Train them so that they have the skills to achieve these new tasks.
- Give them what they earn and deserve so that they don't become spoiled and entitled (putting in the bare minimum of effort and expecting a maximum reward in return).

*(continued)*

(*continued*)

- Accept explanations but not excuses. Focus them on what they can control, even when they would rather hide their shortcomings behind excuses.
- Be available. You cannot influence people if you're aloof.
- Be consistent with all of these steps, whether you feel like it or not. If it's the right thing to do, then put your coffee down, get out of your office, and lead!

Which of these areas do you need to toughen up in? Considering the points made in this rant, here's a fair question: Are you a leader or a nanny? Are your words and deeds consistent? If you talk like a big dog, but walk like a pissant, it's time to raise your game (you could be reaching your leadership sell-by date). If you believe you can do better, then you must.

# Part Four Summary

Getting the team right starts with getting the right people—people who have the talent, drive, attitude, character, energy, and passion to add value to your culture, execute their master the art of execution (MAX) acts with excellence, and contribute meaningfully to the organization's ultimate few objectives (TUFs).

A short list of responsibilities to make this become a reality looks like this:

- Be a leader worth following. Demonstrate the character, competence, consistency, compassion, and commitment others want to follow.
- Stop overmanaging and underleading.
- Create a culture that attracts, develops, and retains the best. Continuously work to improve your five cultural pillars.
- Install the MAX process so that good people have the structure they need to fulfill their potential.
- Turn hiring into an elimination process. Stop making stupid, costly, emotional hiring decisions that everyone must endure day in and day out.
- Stop blaming the lousy people on your team for performance failures, and make sure you're doing your job to train, coach, and mentor them.
- Build relationships that earn higher levels of engagement from your people.
- Face reality and understand whether you're truly hoping or wishing.

- Use the three Ts filter to prune your less-than-optimal performers effectively.
- Stop defending the deadweight and deal with it.
- Don't become a lid on your people. Continue to grow so that you're better able to grow those around you.

There's plenty more to add that will support you in mastering the art of execution, but this will keep you busy for a while. In a nutshell, just *do your job! See? It's not rocket science!*

# About the Author

For more information about Dave Anderson, his seminars, or LearnToLead, visit www.learntolead.com.

For daily business and motivational tips, follow @DaveAnderson100 on Twitter.

If you would like to book Dave to speak with your organization, e-mail Rhonda@learntolead.com or call (818) 735-9503.

Additional books by Dave Anderson and John Wiley & Sons include:

*Up Your Business!: 7 Steps to Fix, Build, or Stretch Your Organization*

*If You Don't Make Waves, You'll Drown: 10 Hard-Charging Strategies for Leading in Politically Correct Times*

*How to Deal with Difficult Customers: 10 Simple Strategies for Selling to the Stubborn, Obnoxious and Belligerent*

*TKO Hiring!: Ten Knockout Strategies for Recruiting, Interviewing, and Hiring Great People*

*TKO Management!: Ten Knockout Strategies for Becoming the Manager Your People Deserve*

*TKO Sales!: Ten Knockout Strategies for Selling More of Anything*

*How to Run Your Business by THE BOOK: A Biblical Blueprint to Bless Your Business*

*How to Lead by THE BOOK: Proverbs, Parables, and Principles to Tackle Your Toughest Business Challenges*

Dave Anderson's LearnToLead and the LearnToLead Elite Center are located in Agoura Hills, California.

# Glossary of Master the Art of Execution Terms

**EDMED:** Every day means every day.

**MAP:** To write the daily lead measure results on the MAX board.

**MAX:** The master the art of execution process.

**MAX act:** A key daily, weekly, or monthly action you take to move toward the TUFs.

**MAX board:** A board where team members post results of their MAX acts from the prior day.

**Prune:** The fifth step of MAX. It means to remove what is undesirable to make room for growth.

**PSP:** A personalized success profile that outlines the daily, weekly, and monthly MAX measures for an individual.

**RAM:** A rhythm of accountability meeting held each morning where each team member reports and records the prior day's MAX act results on the MAX board.

**Realign:** The first stage of pruning. To realign time, resources, talent, et cetera away from things that are good but not great, and into areas that are great or have the potential to become great (things that bring you a diminishing return).

**Revitalize:** The second stage of pruning. To bring back to life unacceptable performances, strategies, processes, et cetera in a last-ditch effort before removing them.

**Remove:** The third stage of pruning. To remove what no longer brings any value (that for which there is no hope).

**TUF:** The ultimate few (goals).

# References

## Introduction

Collins, Jim, and Morten T. Hansen. 2011. *Great by Choice: Uncertainty, Chaos, and Luck—Why Some Thrive despite Them All.* New York: HarperBusiness.

EY. n.d. "Business Redefined—Understanding the Forces Transforming Our World." EY. Accessed April 24, 2015. http://www.ey.com/GL/en/Issues/Business-environment/Business-redefined—Understanding-the-forces-transforming-our-world.

Hay, Maciamo. 2014. "Your Life Is Going to Change Faster Than Ever Before." Life 2.0. April 15. Accessed April 24, 2015. http://www.vitamodularis.org/articles/your_life_is_going_to_change_faster_than_ever_before.shtml.

Meister, Jeanne. 2012. "Job Hopping Is the 'New Normal' for Millennials: Three Ways to Prevent a Human Resource Nightmare." "Leadership" (blog). *Forbes.* August 14. Accessed April 24, 2015. http://www.forbes.com/sites/jeannemeister/2012/08/14/job-hopping-is-the-new-normal-for-millennials-three-ways-to-prevent-a-human-resource-nightmare/.

Regalado, Antonio. 2013. "Technology Is Wiping out Companies Faster Than Ever." *MIT Technology Review.* September 10. Accessed April 24, 2015. http://www.technologyreview.com/view/519226/technology-is-wiping-out-companies-faster-than-ever/.

Robinson, Ken. 2009. Introduction to *The Element: How Finding Your Passion Changes Everything.* With Lou Aronica. New York: Viking. https://books.google.com/books?id=E1N4z9jyzwYC&printsec=frontcover&dq=theelementkenrobinson&hl=en&sa=

X&ei=uKM5VdizIc3FogSkqoDwCw&ved=0CBQQ6AEw
AA#v=onepage&q=ourworldischangingfaster&f=false.

Thomas, Douglas, and John Seely Brown. 2011. *A New Culture of Learning: Cultivating the Imagination for a World of Constant Change.* Lexington, KY: CreateSpace. http://www.newcultureoflearning .com.

Tobak, Steve. 2013. "The Real Impact of Political Correctness." *FOX Business.* April 19. Accessed April 24, 2015. http://www .foxbusiness.com/business-leaders/2013/04/19/real-impact-political-correctness/.

## Part One

BrainyQuote. n.d. "John Wooden Quotes." Accessed April 3, 2015. http://www.brainyquote.com/quotes/authors/j/john_wooden.html.

*Dictionary.com.* n.d. s.v.v. "fray," "priority," and "pruning." Accessed April 3, 2015. http://dictionary.reference.com/.

Manuel, Dai. n.d. "The Top 101 Jim Rohn Quotes of All Time." Dai Manuel: The Moose Is Loose. Accessed April 3, 2015. http:// www.daimanuel.com/2013/12/10/the-top-101-jim-rohn-quotes-of-all-time/.

## Part Two

Collins, Jim. n.d. "Defining Greatness." Accessed April 15, 2015. http://www.jimcollins.com/media_topics/defining.html.

*Dictionary.com.* n.d. s.v.v "apathetic," "denial," "hope," "mediocre," "seduce," and "wish." Accessed April 14, 2015. http://dictionary. reference.com/.

———. n.d. s.v.v. "catalyst," "leadership," and "manage." Accessed April 12, 2015. http://dictionary.reference.com/.

Maxwell, John C. 2013. *The 5 Levels of Leadership: Proven Steps to Maximize Your Potential.* Reprint ed. New York: Center Street.

Whyte, David. 1996. *The Heart Aroused: Poetry and the Preservation of the Soul in Corporate America.* Reissue ed. New York: Crown Business.

## Part Three

*Dictionary.com*. n.d. s.v.v. "blame," "consistent," "earn," "deserve," "excuse," "fault," "mediocre," "mission," "standard," and "suggestion." Accessed April 20, 2015. http://dictionary.reference.com/.

————. n.d. s.v.v. "commit," "complacent," "diligent," "interest," "responsible," "tough-minded," and "sloth." Accessed April 21, 2015. http://dictionary.reference.com/.

IMDb. n.d. "Animal House (1978): Quotes." IMDb. Accessed April 21, 2015. http://www.imdb.com/title/tt0077975/quotes.

## Part Four

BrainyQuote. n.d. "John F. Kennedy Quotes." Accessed April 24, 2015. http://www.brainyquote.com/quotes/quotes/j/johnfkenn110220.html.

*Dictionary.com*. n.d. s.v.v. "attitude," "character," "drive," "energy," "passion," and "teach." Accessed April 24, 2015. http://dictionary.reference.com/.

# Index

# Other Books by Dave Anderson

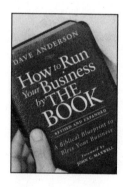

### How to Run Your Business by THE BOOK
### (9781118022375)

*How to Run Your Business by THE BOOK* reveals biblical lessons to help transform the people, culture, and results of your business. Not only will you master timeless business principles based on the world's bestselling book, but you'll also build a foundation for your business that leads to long-term success.

### How to Lead by THE BOOK
### (9780470936283)

*How to Lead by THE BOOK* presents a series of personal and business challenges recognizable to leaders, then deals with each through insight, personal experience, and a discussion of why conventional approaches often fail.

***TKO Management!: Ten Knockout Strategies for Becoming the Manager Your People Deserve (9780470171776)***

***TKO Hiring!: Ten Knockout Strategies for Recruiting, Interviewing, and Hiring Great People (9780470171769)***

***TKO Sales!: Ten Knockout Strategies for Selling More of Anything (9780470171783)***

Dave Anderson's *TKO* series presents no-nonsense, down-in-the-trenches management strategies that work in the real world of business. Each of the three informative books in this series offers easy-to-follow, step-by-step guidance on developing the specific skills great managers need.

### Up Your Business!: 7 Steps to Fix, Build, or Stretch Your Organization, 2nd Edition, Revised and Expanded (9780470068564)

In this newly updated edition of *Up Your Business!*, Anderson lays out a real-world, seven-step program for supercharging any company's performance. Easily adapted to businesses of every size and complexion, the program arms managers and entrepreneurs with proven strategies they can use to fix, build, or stretch their organizations.

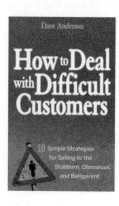

### How to Deal with Difficult Customers: 10 Simple Strategies for Selling to the Stubborn, Obnoxious, and Belligerent (9780470045473)

*How to Deal with Difficult Customers* addresses the question that every serious salesperson eventually deals with—"How do I sell to this jerk?" The book offers 10 brief, easy-to-read, and humorous chapters that cover everything salespeople need to know to deal with customers who make salespeople want to scream.